SOFT SKILLS TRAINING

A workbook to develop skills for employment

Frederick H. Wentz

CONTENTS

CONTENTS

CONTENTS

CONTENTS

CONTENTS

CONTENTS

SOFT SKILLS

SOFT SKILLS

SOFT SKILLS

Soft skills are the nontechnical skills, abilities, and traits that workers need to function in a specific employment environment. They include four sets of workplace competencies:

1. Personal qualities and work ethic

2. Problem-solving and other cognitive skills

3. Oral communication skills

4. Interpersonal and teamwork skills

Wilhelmina Leigh, Deitra H. Lee, and Malinda A. Lindquist

UNIVERSAL HIRING RULE

Any employer will hire any applicant as long as they are convinced that the hiring will bring more value than it costs. It's as simple as that. Employers will hire people they feel will produce value for them.

From *GUERRILLA TACTICS IN THE NEW JOB MARKET* by Tom Jackson, copyright © 1991 by Thomas Jackson. Published by Bantam Books.

EMPLOYMENT NOTES

Three important factors in getting hired are to convince the employer that you are a solution to a problem and not a problem yourself, you will not be more trouble than you are worth, and you will not need to have someone babysit you while you are at work.

Most new hires are excellent employees during their first week on a new job. During the second week, the mature employee will continue to remain focused and continue to improve. The immature employee starts to display all of his or her bad habits, which most often includes laziness, a lack of focus, and disruptive behavior.

THINKING SKILLS 1

1. List five traits or skills you can offer an employer.

A. _____

_____

B. _____

_____

C. _____

_____

D. _____

_____

E. _____

_____

2. In what ways can an employee be more trouble than he or she is worth to an employer?

A. _____

_____

B. _____

_____

C. _____

_____

3. Why would employees need to have someone babysit them while they are at work?

_____

_____

_____

_____

_____

Essential Workplace Traits and Skills

- Dependable and punctual
- Communicate effectively
- Thinking and problem-solving skills
- Taking pride in your work
- Desire to learn
- Ability to get along with others
- Ability to take instructions
- Positive attitude
- Trustworthy and honest
- Respectful
- Ability to control your emotions
- Ability to take constructive criticism
- Friendly
- Helpful
- Conscientious

COMPETENCIES

Effective workers must be able to productively use:

- <u>Resources</u>: allocating time, money, materials, space, and staff

- <u>Interpersonal</u>: working on teams, teaching others, serving customers, leading, negotiating, and working well with people from culturally diverse backgrounds

- <u>Information</u>: acquiring and evaluating data, organizing and maintaining files, interpreting and communicating, and using computers to process information

- <u>Systems</u>: understanding social, organizational, and technological systems, monitoring and correcting performance, and designing or improving systems

- <u>Technology</u>: selecting equipment and tools, applying technology to specific tasks, and maintaining and troubleshooting technologies

Secretary's Commission on Achieving Necessary Skills, U.S. Department of Labor

QUICKLY NOTICED

In the workplace, the lack of soft skills is quickly noticed in people who have neglected to improve them. If you lack soft skills, you might be able to get a job, but you will probably remain in a low-paying job without any advancement and you also increase your chances of getting fired. By learning and developing your soft skills, you are choosing to improve your life. The only trait that you need is the desire to grow as a human being. In order to grow as a human being, you have to be willing to change. If you choose not to change and grow, then look in a mirror because you will remain in the same situation you are in right now, and you will not have the opportunity to enjoy the pleasures that life offers. Remember, not developing your soft skills increases your chances of being unemployed, working in a low-paying job for the rest of your life, consistently being fired, working in a job with no advancement opportunities, and not being able to support your family. There is nothing complicated about this process; it is just a matter of staying focused.

THINKING SKILLS 2

1. List five examples of how an employee displays the lack of soft skills.

A. _____

_____

B. _____

_____

C. _____

_____

D. _____

_____

E. _____

_____

2. When hiring, what traits do you think an employer looks for in an employee?

A. _____
B. _____
C. _____
D. _____
E. _____

THINKING SKILLS 3

RANDOM SQUIGGLES

Here is a line of what appears to be random squiggles. The human mind is built to search for order. Sometimes it finds order that is not really there. Is there any order in this array? If so, what is it and which, if any, of the lettered squiggles should logically be put where the question mark is?

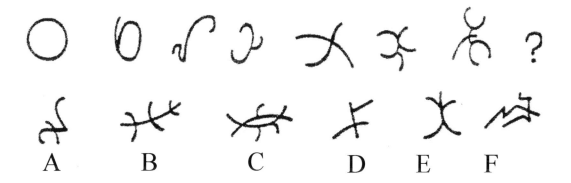

RANDOM SQUIGGLES

This exercise illustrates two very important work-related concepts: the concepts of believing in yourself and not giving up when faced with a challenge. Throughout your life, you will experience situations you have never dealt with before; you will not know what to do, how to do it, how to act, or what to say. The situation will be accompanied by feelings of insecurity. This obstacle holds a lot of people back. They experience something unfamiliar and they stop. They figure that since they do not know anything about the unfamiliar situation, it is better not to attempt something new than to take the risk of looking bad or being embarrassed. After all, it does not feel good to be laughed at or made fun of.

You probably looked at this exercise and had no idea what the answer was. Once you found out the correct answer, it became apparent how easy and logical the answer is. Every obstacle in life is just like random squiggles. The obstacle holding you back might seem impossible to overcome, but if you do not give up, you will eventually figure out a way to overcome the obstacle. You will be able to look back and realize how easy it was to overcome.

When starting a new job, you will come across situations in which you will not know what to do, and you will feel insecure. A lot of employees will shy away from trying something unfamiliar because of the chance of being embarrassed. Remember random squiggles. Don't give up. Accept the challenge. Once you learn how to do the job, you will look back on the situation and realize how easy it was to learn the new task. Every day on a job, you should be more knowledgeable about your job than you were the previous day. The longer you are employed, the easier it will get. Other employees might tease you and laugh at you because you do not know something. Do not respond in a negative manner to being teased. Smile and walk away. They were once in the same situation.

If you do not give up, you can accomplish anything you want. Life is a struggle. Life is difficult. But if you face your struggles and difficulties, and overcome them, you are able to look back and realize that it was not as big of a struggle or as difficult as you first thought it was. It is similar to your first perception of the random squiggles exercise.

Rather than denying problems, focus inventively, intentionally on what solutions might look or feel like...Our mind is meant to generate ideas that help us escape circumstantial traps—if we trust it to do so. Naturally, not all hunches are useful. But then you only need a single good idea to solve a problem.
—Marsha Sinetar

Stand up to your obstacles and do something about them. You will find that they haven't half the strength you think they have.
—Norman Vincent Peale

'NEVER GIVE UP!'

Winston Churchill was a great man who failed the sixth grade, and was defeated in every election for public office until he became Prime Minister at the young age of 62.

Sir Winston Churchill took three years getting through eighth grade because he had trouble learning English. He suffered from a speech impediment, and had great difficulty pronouncing the letter "s." It seems ironic that years later Oxford University asked him to address its commencement exercises.

He arrived with his usual props. A cigar, a cane and a top hat accompanied Churchill wherever he went. As Churchill approached the podium, the crowd rose in appreciated applause. With unmatched dignity, he settled the crowd and stood confident before his admirers. Removing the cigar and carefully placing the top hat on the podium, Churchill gazed at his waiting audience. Authority rang in Churchill's voice as he shouted, "Never give up!"

Several seconds passed before he rose to his toes and repeated: "Never give up!" His words thundered in their ears. There was a deafening silence as Churchill reached for his hat and cigar, steadied himself with his cane and left the platform. His commencement address was finished.

Because Winston Churchill never gave up, he is now remembered as one of the greatest world leaders of the twentieth century.

Reprinted with permission from Mitchell Earl Gibson, MD, *NINE INSIGHTS FOR A HAPPY LIFE*

EMPLOYMENT NOTES

If your new job is physically and mentally challenging, or your new boss is a jerk, or it is hard to relate to your coworkers, don't give up. After a couple of weeks, your mind and body will adapt and things will be much easier. Your boss will still be a jerk, but just accept it and perform your job.

EMPLOYMENT NOTES

If you keep telling yourself that your job is too hard, then your job is going to be hard. If you tell yourself that your job is easy, then your job will be easy.

IN EACH OF OUR LIVES

In each of our lives, for whatever reason, there are times that we are faced with things that just don't make sense to us. And the more we struggle to understand our hardships, the less any of it makes sense.

I have found that in every challenge and obstacle that we are faced with, there *can* be good that can come from it! While it's almost never easy to identify, I assure you that it is there lying dormant just waiting for us to release it! I urge everyone to spend your days looking for positives in your life.

Reprinted with permission from Josh Hinds

WHEN WE SAY
Dr. Penelope Russianoff

When we say "I can't do it, whether it be carry a tune, face a job interview, or initiate a conversation, the words go from our mouths into our ears and then to our brains, where they stick. Saying is believing. "I'm a failure. I'm stupid. I have no talent. And I never will. I can't change." The very sound of our voice confirms the verdict. How much better for our ears to hear, and our brains to register, "Yes, I can change. I can at least do my best to change. I can try."

Emerson tells us, "A man is what he thinks all day long." If we spend our days wallowing in feelings of helplessness, inferiority, or anxiety, then we are helpless, inferior, and anxious. If, on the other hand we elect to change, we have taken the first indispensable step towards ending these losing games. Maybe a psychotic cannot change, or someone missing a Y chromosome, or a drug burnout. But for the rest of us garden-variety troubled human beings, the door to change is always open. We just have to choose to walk through it.

LIFE IS DIFFICULT

Life is difficult.

This is a great truth, one of the greatest truths. It is a great truth because once we truly see this truth, we transcend it. Once we truly know that life is difficult—once we truly understand and accept it—then life is no longer difficult. Because once it is accepted, the fact that life is difficult no longer matters.

THE WORK OF ADULT LIFE

The work of adult life is not easy. As in childhood, each step presents not only new tasks of development but requires a letting go of techniques that worked before. With each passage some magic must be given up, some cherished illusion of safety and comfortably familiar sense of self must be cast off, to allow for the greater expansion of our own distinctiveness.

From *PASSAGES,* by Gail Sheehy, copyright © 1974, 1976, renewed 2004 by Gail Sheehy. Published by Ballantine Books.

IT WOULD BE SURPRISING

It would be surprising if we didn't experience some pain as we leave the familiarity of one adult stage for the uncertainty of the next. But the willingness to move through each passage is equivalent to the willingness to live abundantly. If we don't change, we don't grow. If we don't grow, we are not really living. Growth demands a temporary surrender of security.

THINKING SKILLS 4

Explain the following sentences:

1. As in childhood, each step presents not only new tasks of development but requires a letting go of techniques that worked before.

_____

_____

_____

_____

2. If we don't change, we don't grow.

_____

_____

_____

_____

3. If we don't grow, we are not really living.

_____

_____

_____

_____

4. Once we truly know that life is difficult—once we truly understand and accept it—then life is no longer difficult.

_____

_____

_____

_____

THINKING SKILLS 5

Can you find the odd one out between these five cubes?

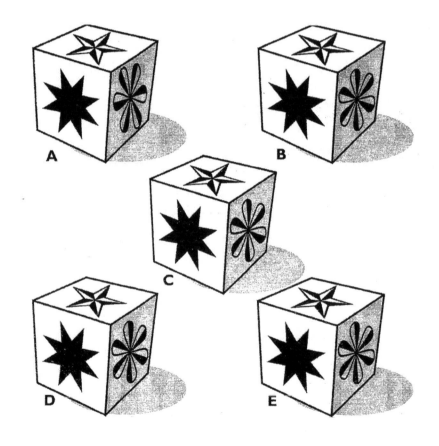

Answer: _____

MENSA MIND BUSTERS, by Philip Carter, Ken Russell, and John Bremmer, © 1999, 2002 by Carlton Books Limited. Published by Thunder Bay Press, an imprint of the Advantage Publishing Group. Reprinted with permission from Carlton Books, Ltd.

3 STRATEGIES FOR CHANGING THE DIRECTION OF YOUR LIFE
Joyce Weiss

STRATEGY 1: PUT THOUGHTS INTO ACTION

We all face challenges in life. Sometimes these challenges keep us stuck in unhappy situations. These predicaments can include burnout, illness, boredom, unhealthy relationships, low self-esteem, divorce, competition, and financial changes, just to name a few. Remember, we choose how we cope with challenges. Different people react differently to similar situations, some better than others.

17th century French philosopher and writer Voltaire compared life to a game in which each player must accept the cards dealt. Once in hand, each player can decide how to play those cards to win the game. Shakespeare said, "Life breaks all of us. Some of us get stronger at the breaks."

We can choose to dwell on our problems or go on with life. Take time to mourn a loss: a loved one who died, a lost job, a relationship or marriage torn apart, or any other significant change in your life. We need a certain amount of time to heal. It is important to deal with the stages of loss and then move on.

STRATEGY 2: ACCEPT RESPONSIBILITY

We have the ability to choose our responses to difficult situations. It is our choice whether we live a boring, unfulfilled, miserable life or a life full of joy, contentment, and growth.

Some people blame their parents, boss, mate, environment, and so forth. They don't accept responsibility for their own lives. A familiar meditation from a 16th century monk states, "Grant me the serenity to accept the things I cannot change, the courage to change the things I can, and the wisdom to know the difference." Some individuals find it easier to complain and blame. Here is a simple effective question to those who dwell on negative situations and don't accept responsibility. Ask them, "Now that you recognize the problem, what are you going to do about it?"

After I earned my Masters Degree in Guidance and Counseling, many people called on me to complain about their partner or job. I listened and empathized, until I realized that many were bright, loving people who complained for years but never made any changes. I began to respond with, "I've listened and you have a legitimate complaint. Now, my question to you is, what are you going to do about it?" A lot of phone calls ceased. It was no longer fun for the complainers to look to other people for solutions. It is vitally important as spouses, friends, and parents to tell the important people in our lives what they need to hear, not what they want to hear.

While presenting a workshop to a Fortune 500 company, management told me what they tell all new employees. They suggest that new employees look at constructive feedback as a gift and not become defensive or insecure about it. What an incredible message! Accepting responsibility for your actions and moving on when you feel stuck are two important lessons to learn when dealing with a challenge.

STRATEGY 3: ACCEPT DIFFERENCES IN OTHERS

Learning to accept differences in others without judging them is another vital lesson. You might be thinking, "I'm a fair person, I don't judge people." But have you ever caught yourself saying things like:

> You should have known better.
> I can't believe you did that!
> Why did you quit your job when you had all those benefits?
> How could you possibly get involved with that person?
> What do you mean you don't drink?
> Chill out and join the party!
> How disgusting!

These are examples of subtle and not-so-subtle ways of judging others. The minute words like *should*, *could*, or *why* creep into the conversation, look out! These words say: "Be like me, because different from me is wrong!" Pay close attention to your words. Work to become nonjudgmental. Begin to learn the importance of taking action, accepting responsibility, and accepting differences.

FULL SPEED AHEAD: BECOME DRIVEN BY CHANGE, by Joyce Weiss, copyright © 1996 by Joyce Weiss. Reprinted with permission from Joyce Weiss.

IQ PREDICTS SUCCESS?

There are widespread exceptions to the rule that IQ predicts success. . . . At best, IQ contributes about 20 percent to the factors that determine life success, which leaves 80 percent to other forces.

. . . these "other characteristics," emotional intelligence: abilities such as being able to motivate oneself and persist in the face of frustrations, to control impulse and delay gratification, to regulate one's moods and keep distress from swamping the ability to think, to empathize and to hope.

THE 11 KEYS TO SUCCESS
Julie Jansen

Observing people in the workplace has yielded 11 keys to success. Time and again, it is apparent that those individuals who exhibit these 11 keys and use them most productively are consistently the most successful and well-liked individuals overall. The good news is that most people are born with at least some of these keys or learned them at a very young age, and all of these keys can be developed or learned later in life.

These are the 11 keys to success:

1. **Confidence:** an unshakable belief in oneself based on a realistic understanding of one's circumstances; a trait that most people admire in others and strive to acquire themselves.

2. **Curiosity:** being eager to know and learn; always showing interest and giving special attention to the less obvious; always being the person who says, "I want to know more about…"

3. **Decisiveness:** arriving at a final conclusion or making a choice and taking action; making decisions with determination even when you don't have all the information you think you need.

4. **Empathy:** demonstrating caring and understanding of someone else's situation, feelings and motives; always thinking about what it's like to walk in someone else's shoes.

5. **Flexibility:** being capable of change; responding positively to change; being pliable, adaptable, non-rigid and able to deal with ambiguity.

6. **Humor:** viewing yourself and the world with enjoyment; not taking life or yourself too seriously; being amusing, amused and, at times, even comical.

7. **Intelligence:** thinking and working smartly and cleverly; being sharp in your dealings; "not reinventing the wheel"; planning before acting; working efficiently and focusing on quality over quantity. (Important note: This is different from IQ, the common abbreviation for intelligence quotient.)

8. **Optimism:** expecting the best possible outcome and dwelling on the most hopeful or positive aspects of a situation; believing that the glass is half full rather than half empty.

9. **Perseverance:** having passion, energy, focus and the desire to get results. Motivation, persistence and hard work are all aspects of perseverance.

10. **Respect:** remembering that it is just as easy to be nice; protecting another person's self-esteem; treating others in a considerate and courteous manner.

11. **Self-awareness:** a sophisticated form of consciousness that enables you to regulate yourself by monitoring yourself, observing yourself and changing your thought processes and behaviors.

Which of these keys are among your strengths? Which of the 11 are among your weaknesses? Self-awareness, the 11th key, is really the foundation for understanding yourself. If you are not sure how self-aware you are, ask several people whom you trust which of these 11 keys they believe are your strengths and which are not. Again, while no one person possesses all of these keys in equal amounts, each of them can be developed and improved.

I DON'T KNOW WHAT I WANT, BUT I KNOW IT'S NOT THIS, by Julie Jansen, copyright 2010 by Julie Jansen, Reprinted with permission from Julie Jansen.

TO KEEP A JOB, YOU MUST BE MATURE ENOUGH TO:

- Not respond in a negative manner to criticism from a supervisor.
- Not respond in a negative manner if you get yelled at by a supervisor.
- Walk away from a confrontation with a fellow employee.
- Take and follow instructions.
- Follow all company rules.
- Do more work than what you are paid for.
- Respect company property and equipment.
- Not steal.
- Be at work every day you are scheduled.
- Work hard when you don't feel like it.
- Not be manipulated by peer pressure.
- Control your emotions.
- Be a leader and not a follower.
- Have a positive attitude at work when things are going wrong in your personal life.
- Be dependable and trustworthy.
- Get along with other employees. (You don't have to like them, but you do have to be professional enough to be pleasant with them.)
- Respect the chain of command.

WHAT IS MATURITY?
Ann Landers

Maturity is the ability to control anger and settle differences without violence or destruction.

Maturity is patience. It is the willingness to pass up immediate pleasures in favor of long-term gains.

Maturity is perseverance, the ability to sweat out a project or a situation in spite of heavy opposition and discouraging setbacks.

Maturity is the capacity to face unpleasantness and frustration, discomfort and defeat, without complaint or collapse.

Maturity is humility. It is being big enough to say, "I was wrong." And, when right, the mature person need not experience the satisfaction of saying, "I told you so."

Maturity is the ability to make a decision and stand by it. The immature spend their lives exploring endless possibilities; then they do nothing.

Maturity means dependability, keeping one's word, coming through in a crisis. The immature are masters of the alibi. They are the confused and disorganized. Their lives are a maze of broken promises, former friends, unfinished business and good intentions that somehow never materialize.

Maturity is the art of living in peace with that which we cannot change, the courage to change that which should be changed and the wisdom to know the difference.

THE BEGINNING OF MATURITY
Dr. Penelope Russianoff

The beginning of maturity in our lives is the recognition that there is no one magic way, that there are endless ways of dealing with the same set of facts. Maturity means accepting responsibility for ourselves and finding our own solutions. Yes, we say we want personal freedom, but freedom means choices and choices are tough to make. No one can hand us the answers. Look at what happened to people who blindly followed Hitler in Nazi Germany, a leader who claimed to have found *The Way*. We need the courage to think for ourselves and overthrow the tyranny of ideas that don't make sense or do not work for us. Until we can do so, we will go around desperately clutching our insecurity blankets, lugging an albatross around, or feeling depressed, angry, or rejected because the culture told us we should feel that way. We will keep on playing those losing games and losing.

From *WHEN AM I GOING TO BE HAPPY? HOW TO BREAK THE EMOTIONAL BAD HABITS THAT MAKE YOU MISERABLE*, by Penelope Russianoff and Joseph E. Persico, copyright © 1988 by Penelope Russianoff and Joseph E. Persico. Reprinted with permission from Bantam Books, a division of Random House, Inc

WHAT DOES 'TAKING PRIDE IN YOUR WORK' MEAN?

- When you finish a job, no matter how simple and easy, you know in your heart that you gave it all of your effort.
- Being able to admire your work when you are finished.
- Doing a job better than anyone else could without being boastful.
- Working under a lot of pressure and stress and still being able to respond in a positive manner to customers or coworkers.
- Being conscientious when you are tired.
- Doing quality work when nobody is watching.
- Making every small job you do important.
- Realizing that the most menial jobs in a business are important.
- Always striving to be the most productive worker.
- Being dependable: never missing work.
- Creating a friendly work atmosphere for other employees.
- Helping other less experienced employees.
- Not decreasing your productivity because you do not think you are paid enough.
- Setting your own work standards.
- Not giving in to peer pressure.
- Developing solutions to workplace problems.
- Being part of the solution and not part of the problem.
- Correcting your own mistakes.
- Always trying to improve.
- Learning on your own.
- Being kind and understanding to other employees.

THINKING SKILLS 6

1. Give three examples of how you can take pride in your work.

A. _____

B. _____

C. _____

2. List the following five positions in a chain of command, with letter "A" being the highest: front line employee, manager, president, supervisor, and owner.

A. _____

B. _____

C. _____

D. _____

E. _____

3. Name three things effective workers must be able to productively use and give an example of each.

A. _____

B. _____

C. _____

THINKING SKILLS 7

Can you find the two sides on these cubes that contain the same letter?

Side_____ & Side_____

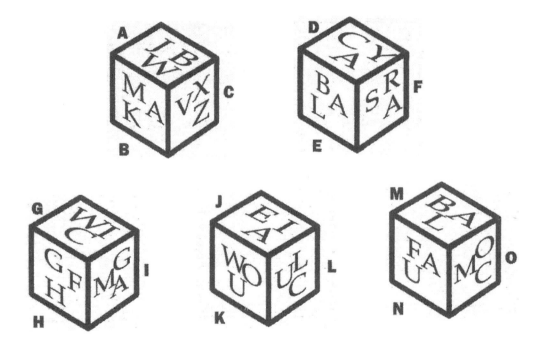

QUOTES FOR DISCUSSION

Most people make use of the first part of their life to render the last part miserable.

—Jean De La Bruyere (1645–1696)

Art is long, life short, judgment difficult, opportunity transient. To act is easy, to think is hard; to act according to our thought is troublesome.

—Goethe, Wilhelm Meister's Apprenticeship, The Harvard Classics Shelf of Fiction (1917)

The snake which cannot cast its skin has to die. As well the minds which are prevented from changing their opinions; they cease to be mind.

—Friedrich Nietzsche (1844–1900)

If men are, for a long time, accustomed only to one sort or method of thought, their minds grow stiff in it, and do not readily turn to another method of thought. I do not propose a variety and stock of knowledge, but a variety and freedom of thinking.

—John Locke (1632–1704)

Life is a series of natural and spontaneous changes. Don't resist them—that only creates sorrow. Let reality be reality. Let things flow naturally forward in whatever way they like.

—Lao Tzu (600 BC)

He who labors diligently need never despair; for all things are accomplished by diligence and labor.

—Menander of Athens (342 BC–292 BC)

You were born with wings. Why prefer to crawl through life?

—Jalal ad-Din Rumi (1207–1273)

Make the most of yourself, for that is all there is of you.

—Ralph Waldo Emerson (1803–1882)

OUR DEEPEST FEAR
Marianne Williamson

Our deepest fear is not that we are inadequate.
Our deepest fear in that we are powerful beyond measure.
It is our Light, not our Darkness, that most frightens us.
We ask ourselves, who am I to be brilliant, gorgeous, talented, and fabulous?
Actually, who are you not to be?
Your playing small does not serve the World.
There is nothing enlightening about shrinking so that other people won't feel unsure around you.
We were born to make manifest the glory that is within us.
It is not just in some of us; it is in everyone.
As we let our own Light shine,
we consciously give other people permission to do the same.
As we are liberated from our own fear,
our presence automatically liberates others.

Quote from pp. 190–191, from *A RETURN TO LOVE* by Marianne Williamson. Copyright © 1992 by Marianne Williamson. Reprinted with permission from HarperCollins Publishers. Portions reprinted from A COURSE IN MIRACLES. Copyrighted © 1975 by Foundation for Inner Peace, Inc. All chapter openings are from *A COURSE IN MIRACLES*.

TIPS TO RAISE YOUR SELF-ESTEEM

1. Practice positive self-talk. Say good things to yourself and think good thoughts about yourself. Focus on your strengths and on a personal commitment to change.

2. Don't compare yourself to others. Forgive yourself. Believe in yourself. Smile.

3. Focus on the positive. Avoid negative people. Associate with positive, supporting friends.

4. Do things that you can be proud of. Do kind acts for others on a daily basis. Congratulate yourself every time you do something kind for someone. Learn to accept compliments.

5. Develop positive qualities that you admire in others. Constantly focus on these qualities during your daily routine. Become aware of your negative thoughts and beliefs, and adjust your thinking to become more positive.

EMPLOYMENT NOTES

A supervisor has less patience than a teacher and is less tolerant of immature behavior. A supervisor is responsible for making sure all the employees are performing the job they are paid for. The employees are paid to do a job so the company can make a profit and keep the employees working. If you are disrespectful, loud, abrasive, emotional, moody, or lazy, you won't be sent to the principal's office, you will be fired and sent home.

THINKING SKILLS 8

1. How does one "play small" on a job?

_____

_____

_____

_____

_____

2. Write down five qualities you admire in others.

A. _____

B. _____

C. _____

D. _____

E. _____

REPRESENTATIVE STUDIES OF EMPLOYER NEEDS
Gary Natriello

Studies of employer needs have been conducted in a variety of businesses and locations with particular purposes in mind; the basic format is generally the same. Employers are in some way asked to express their need for personnel.

Although it is not possible to review all of the studies of this type, examining a representative group of studies of employers' expressed needs provides sufficient background for considering the quality of the evidence they present regarding the demands of the modern workplace. Below is a brief summary of some of the findings:

Employers were asked to identify employee skills requiring more emphasis:
1. Dependability received the highest rating
2. Basic communication
3. Thinking and problem solving
4. Basic arithmetic

Employers were asked what the reasons were for rejecting entry-level job applications:
1. Low interest
2. Previous job hopping
3. Poor communication skills

Employers were asked the most common reasons for termination:
1. Absenteeism
2. Lack of interest

Employers were asked about areas in which employees need to improve:
1. Concern for productivity
2. Pride in work
3. Responsibility

Employers were asked about characteristics that affected employee selection:
1. Communication skills
2. Appearance
3. Stable work experience
4. Self-confidence
5. Interviewing skills
6. Desire to learn
7. Accurate application
8. Grammar
9. The desire to advance

Employers were asked what entry-level workers lacked:
1. Basic skills in math, reading, and writing.
2. Career goals
3. Enthusiasm for the job

Employers rated the importance of 64 identified attributes for entry-level success and advancement:
1. Positive work attitudes
2. Thinking skills
3. Ability to learn

Employers were asked how they recruit and hire:
1. Dependability
2. Proper attitude
3. Good team member
4. Basic adult literacy

Educators and especially employers stressed the need for youth to develop:
1. Proper attitudes about work
2. Realistic expectations about job content and wages
3. Basic skills

Employers were asked what was most important for advancement:
1. Ability to learn
2. Thinking skills

Employers were asked what work attitudes were most important:
1. Trustworthiness and flexibility
2. Appearance
3. Respectfulness
4. Cooperativeness

Employers were asked about areas in which entry-level employees needed the most improvement
1. Attitude
2. Attendance
3. Punctuality
4. Appearance
5. Communication skills

Natriello, G., *What Do Employers Want in Entry-Level Workers? An Assessment of the Evidence.* National Center for Education and Employment Occasional Paper No. 7

THINKING SKILLS 9

1. What employee skills require more emphasis?

A. _____

B. _____

C. _____

2. What were the most common reasons for termination?

A. _____

B. _____

3. What do most entry-level workers lack?

A. _____

B. _____

C. _____

4. In what areas do entry-level employees need the most improvement?

A. _____

B. _____

C. _____

D. _____

E. _____

Survey After Survey
Gary Natriello

Survey after survey of employers who hire entry-level workers reveal how important it is for job candidates to have soft skills. In *Job Prospects for Welfare Recipients: Employers Speak Out*, researchers found that a positive attitude and dependability are the two qualities that employers identify as most important when hiring someone for entry-level work (Regenstein et al., July 1998). *Problems with interpersonal and other soft skills are a major barrier to employment that employers do not believe they can address on their own* (Welfare to Work Partnership, 2000).

In a summary of 14 studies on the needs expressed by employers for entry-level job qualifications, Dr. Gary Natriello found that:

1) Employers place greatest importance on employee attitudes,

2) Employers emphasize basic skills over job-specific skills, and

3) Employers deem it important for workers to have an understanding of the work environment.

Natriello, G., *What Do Employers Want in Entry-Level Workers? An Assessment of the Evidence.* National Center for Education and Employment Occasional Paper No. 7

DEPENDABLE EMPLOYEES

- You can be the hardest worker, but if you are not dependable you are not worth much to the employer.
- If you are not dependable, you will be expendable.
- A dependable employee is always at work when he or she is scheduled.
- It takes a lot of sacrifice to be a dependable employee.
- A dependable employee is honest and trustworthy.
- When a person misses work, the other employees have to work a lot harder.
- A person who is always missing work is sending a signal to the manager that they do not care about his or her job.
- A dependable employee is valuable to any company.
- If you are not at work when you are needed, then you will not be needed.
- Employees who are not dependable do not understand why they get fired.
- Dependable employees receive better treatment from management.
- Employees who are not dependable do not understand this and will accuse management of favoritism.
- If you were a manager, wouldn't you give the best schedule to your most dependable employees?
- Dependable employees are treated better because the company does not want to lose them.

THE SURVEY SAYS
Daniel Goleman

In a national survey of what employers are looking for in entry-level workers, specific technical skills are now less important than the underlying ability to learn on the job. Employers listed the following:

Ability to learn on the job

Listening and oral communication

Adaptability and creative responses to setbacks and obstacles

Personal management, confidence, motivation to work toward goals, a sense of wanting to develop one's career and take pride in accomplishments

Group and interpersonal effectiveness, cooperativeness and teamwork, skills at negotiating disagreements

Effectiveness in the organization, wanting to make a contribution, leadership potential

Competence in reading, writing, and math

Of the seven desired traits, just one was academic: competence in reading, writing, and math.

THINKING SKILLS 10

These shapes are all different, but there is a principle behind their arrangement. Which of the lettered shapes in the line below logically goes where the question mark is?

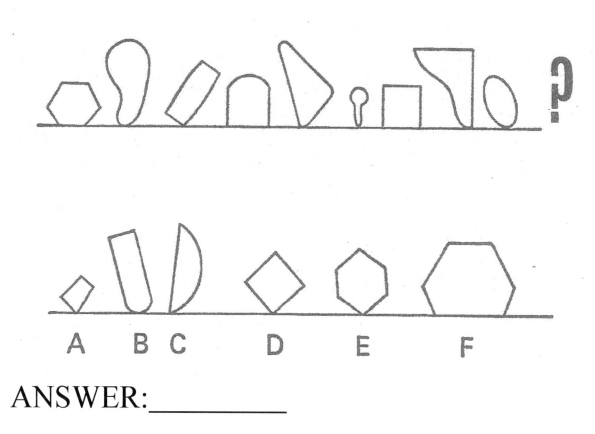

ANSWER:_____

I Hope This Upsets You, SEREBRIAKOFF, VICTOR, *PUZZLES, PROBLEMS AND PASTIMES FOR THE SUPERINTELLIGENT*, 1ˢᵗ Edition, ©1983, p.36. Reprinted with permission from Pearson Educational, Inc., Upper Saddle River, NJ.

TRAINING AND ADVANCEMENT

Workers prepare for employment in many ways, but the most fundamental form of job training in the United States is a high school education. Better than 88 percent of the Nation's workforce possessed a high school diploma or its equivalent in 2004. However, many occupations require more training, so growing numbers of workers pursue additional training or education after high school. In 2004, 28.7 percent of the Nation's workforce reported having completed some college or an associate's degree as their highest level of education, while an additional 29.5 percent continued in their studies and attained a bachelor's or higher degree. In addition to these types of formal education, other sources of qualifying training include formal company-provided training, apprenticeships, informal on-the-job training, correspondence courses, Armed Forces vocational training, and non-work-related training.

Persons with no more than a high school diploma accounted for about 64.7 percent of all workers in construction; 64.3 in agriculture, forestry, fishing, and hunting; 60.7 percent in accommodation and food services; 60.4 percent in mining; 51.5 percent in manufacturing; and 50.6 in retail trade. On the other hand, those who had acquired a bachelor's or higher degree accounted for 63.2 percent of all workers in private educational services; 60.6 percent in professional, scientific, and technical services; 43.4 percent in finance and insurance; and 42.0 percent in information.

Education and training also are important factors in the variety of advancement paths found in different industries. Each industry has some unique advancement paths, but workers who complete additional on-the-job training or education generally help their chances of being promoted. In much of the manufacturing sector, for example, production workers who receive training in management and computer skills increase their likelihood of being promoted to supervisory positions. Other factors that impact advancement and that may figure prominently in the industries covered in the Career Guide include the size of the establishments, institutionalized career tracks, and the mix of occupations. As a result, persons who seek jobs in particular industries should be aware of how these advancement paths and other factors may later shape their careers.

Source: Bureau of Labor Statistics

THINKING SKILLS 11

1. What is the most fundamental form of job training in the United States?

   _____

2. Do a lot of occupations require more training than a high school education?

   _____

3. Which industry accounts for the highest percentage of workers with no more than a high school education?

   _____

4. What are some other sources of job-related qualified training?

   A. _____

   B. _____

   C. _____

   D. _____

THE SILENT EPIDEMIC
John M. Bridgeland, John J. DiIulio, Jr., and Karen Burke Morison

There is a high school dropout epidemic in America. Each year, almost one third of all public high school students—and nearly one half of all Blacks, Hispanics and Native Americans—fail to graduate from public high school with their class. Many of these students abandon school with less than two years to complete their high school education. This *tragic cycle* has not substantially improved during the past few decades when education reform has been high on the public agenda. During this time, the public has been almost entirely unaware of the severity of the dropout problem due to inaccurate data. The consequences remain tragic. The decision to drop out is a dangerous one for the student. Dropouts are much more likely than their peers who graduate to be unemployed, living in poverty, receiving public assistance, in prison, on death row, unhealthy, divorced, and single parents with children who drop out from high school themselves.

The Silent Epidemic: Perspectives of High School Dropouts
A report by Civic Enterprises in association with Peter D. Hart Research Associates
for the Bill & Melinda Gates Foundation
By: John M. Bridgeland, John J. DiIulio, Jr., Karen Burke Morison
March 2006

THINKING SKILLS 12

1. What percentage of high school students drop out before graduation?

_____

2. What percentage of all Blacks, Hispanics, and Native Americans fail to graduate?

_____

3. Finish the following sentence:
Dropouts are much more likely than their peers who graduated to be _____

_____

_____

_____

_____

4. Why do you think that most dropouts are most likely to be unemployed?_____

_____

_____

_____

_____

TRAGIC CYCLE

The tragic cycle refers to generation after generation of individuals following down the same path of self-destruction. When a young person grows up in a neighborhood with older adults who are involved in drugs, alcohol, violence, and killings, he or she thinks this is normal and is what life is all about. A lot of times this young person ends up being just like the adults he or she saw while growing up. There comes a point in your life where you have to take responsibility for the damage done to you by misguided adults and your community. You have to accept and correct this damage. Nobody is going to help you break this cycle but yourself. The way to break this cycle is through education. It will be worth it.

EMPLOYMENT NOTES

There is a cycle you can break once you start working—the cycle of being afraid to excel, holding yourself back by not performing up to your potential, and basing your performance on the performance of the other employees. Employees who work like all the other employees are paid like all the other employees. Employees who perform more work than other employees are eventually paid more, receive better treatment, and have more opportunities for advancement.

MAINSPRINGS OF SELF-EXCELLENCE
S. A. Swami, Ph.D.

1. Self-confidence

2. Planned continuous learning

3. Commitment and willingness to work

4. Motivation and enthusiasm

5. Willingness to forego immediate pleasures

6. Emotion management

7. Reaching out to help others

SELF-EXCELLENCE: KEY TO PREVENTIVE STRESS MANAGEMENT & GOAL ORIENTED LIVING, by S. A. Swami, Ph.D., Published by Minibook Publishing Co. Reprinted with permission from Mrs. Swami.

THINKING SKILLS 13

1. What is meant by the term "tragic cycle"?

_____

_____

_____

_____

_____

_____

2. Explain in one word how this cycle is broken?

_____

3. How do you take responsibility for your life?

_____

_____

_____

4. Why is it important to reach out and help others while at work?

_____

_____

_____

_____

THINKING SKILLS 14

1. Can you name three consecutive days without using the words Sunday, Wednesday, or Friday?

_____

2. Would you rather a bear attack you or a tiger?

_____

3. You are participating in a race. You overtake the second person. What position are you in?

_____

4. If yesterday was Thursday, what day is three days before the day after tomorrow?

_____

5. What is the largest amount of money you can have in change and still not have change for a dollar bill?

_____

QUOTES FOR DISCUSSION

If a man neglects education, he walks lame to the end of his life.

—Plato (429 BC–347 BC)

Without education, you're not going anywhere in this world.

—Malcolm X (1925–1965)

The roots of education are bitter, but the fruit is sweet.

—Aristotle (384 BC–322 BC)

The only person who is educated is the one who has learned how to learn and change.

—Chinese proverb

The only thing more expensive than education is ignorance.

—Benjamin Franklin (1706–1790)

Only the educated are free.

—Epictetus (55 AD–135 AD)

There is only one good, knowledge, and one evil, ignorance.

—Socrates (469 BC–399 BC)

It is only the ignorant who despise education.

—Publilius Syrus (first century BC)

Ignorant men raise questions that wise men answered a thousand years ago.

—Johann Wolfgang von Goeth (1749–1832)

Education is our passport to the future, for tomorrow belongs to the people who prepare for it today.

—Malcolm X (1925–1965)

EVERY HUMAN BEING IS DIFFERENT

There is no such thing as a stupid person. Every human being is different. Some individuals are better at certain subjects than others, but every person has the ability to learn. A big difference-maker is moral support and the development of self-confidence and self-esteem early in life. Once you realize that you have the ability to learn and be successful, it is easier to apply yourself and not give up.

Some people give up on school because adults in their lives always put them down, offer no support, call them names such as "stupid," and damage their self-confidence and self-esteem. It becomes a self-fulfilling prophecy. Not learning basic knowledge at a young age can limit future advancement and create an anti-educational attitude.

If you are behind in your education and learning, the positive side is that it is never too late to catch up and increase access to better opportunities in life. It is more than just saying that you are going to learn how to read better, get better grades, or get your GED. You have to constantly focus on what you want to accomplish and put in the work. You have to study every day, not mind what others say, and not be embarrassed to admit your deficiency. It amounts to a lot of hard work, effort, and sacrifice. It is not something you can do part-time or just when you feel like it. You will have to sacrifice your social life on a temporary basis if you want to improve your long-term chances of success.

Employment opportunities will be limited without a good education. Advancement opportunities will be limited without a good education. Being behind in your reading skills will limit you even further. I use the phrase of "being behind" because with dedication and hard work, anybody can improve and catch up.

If you can't read, it's going to be hard to realize dreams.

—Booker T. Washington (1856–1915)

CHILDREN LEARN WHAT THEY LIVE
Dorothy Law Nolte

If children live with criticism, they learn to condemn.

If children live with hostility, they learn to fight.

If children live with fear, they learn to be apprehensive.

If children live with pity, they learn to feel sorry for themselves.

If children live with ridicule, they learn to feel shy.

If children live with jealousy, they learn to feel envy.

If children live with shame, they learn to feel guilty.

If children live with encouragement, they learn confidence.

If children live with tolerance, they learn patience.

If children live with praise, they learn appreciation.

If children live with acceptance, they learn to love.

If children live with approval, they learn to like themselves.

If children live with recognition, they learn it is good to have a goal.

If children live with sharing, they learn generosity.

If children live with honesty, they learn truthfulness.

If children live with fairness, they learn justice.

If children live with kindness and consideration, they learn respect.

If children live with security, they learn to have faith in themselves and in those about them.

If children live with friendliness, they learn the world is a nice place in which to live.

WHAT IS IGNORANCE?

- Thinking you know everything
- Negelecting your education
- Not caring
- Living life day to day
- Believeing things will get better without effort
- Putting other people down
- Not being kind and considerate of others
- Wanting a pay raise without putting in the work
- Using violence as a problem-solving technique
- Having no priorities or goals
- Not trying to improve yourself
- Thinking you do not have the ability to learn
- Not realizing you are just as important as anyone else
- Feeling that you are unlucky
- Treating others like you would not want to be treated
- Not thinking in terms of consequences
- Feeling that you are owed something
- Losing touch with your feelings
- Neglecting your communication skills
- Not foregoing immediate pleasures
- Unwilling to learn and change
- Getting angry and responding without thinking
- Stealing from an employer
- Being materialistic

WHEN A TREE IS UPROOTED
Thubten Chodron

When a tree is uprooted, its branches wither and die. Similarly, once ignorance is totally eliminated, anger, attachment, jealousy, arrogance, fear, and anxiety can no longer arise because they are all rooted in ignorance. When these afflictions cease, contaminated actions no longer are created, thus the suffering that they cause ceases forever. That's why understanding emptiness, the correct view, is so important: It's the direct antidote to the very root of all unsatisfactory circumstances. By deepening that view and familiarizing our minds more and more with reality, we purify the mind.

HOW TO FREE YOUR MIND, TARA THE LIBERATOR, by Thubten Chodron, copyright © 2005 by Thubten Chodron. Published by Snow Lion Publication. Reprinted with permission from Snow Lion Publication.

80 PERCENT OF PRISONERS IN AMERICA ARE HIGH SCHOOL DROPOUTS

Statistics on the economic disparity between those who have completed high school and those who have dropped out, and the related social implications of this disparity, are troubling. In 2000, an estimated 11 percent of 16- through 24-year-olds who were not enrolled in a high school program had neither a high school diploma nor an equivalent credential (U.S. GAO, 2002). In 1993, more than 12 million people 18 years or older possessed less than a ninth-grade education (National Dropout Prevention Network, 2000). High school graduates earn an average of $6,415 more per year than those who drop out. In 1998, 28.2 percent of youths in the labor force who had dropped out of school in the previous 12 months were unemployed. In comparison, the unemployment rate of 1998 high school graduates who were not enrolled in college was much lower at 18.4 percent (Bureau of Labor Statistics, 1999). A National Center for Education Statistics study found that in 1994, high school dropouts were more than twice as likely to receive public assistance as high school graduates who did not go on to college—14 percent compared to 6 percent (Smith et al., 1996). High school dropouts also comprise a disproportionate share of the nation's prisons and death row inmates (U.S. GAO, 2002). Eighty percent of prisoners in America are high school dropouts, according to the National Dropout Prevention Network (2000) study of *Dropout Statistics.*

EMPLOYMENT NOTES

Ignorance is not permanent. It is a choice we make. The world is full of ignorant people. You will be surrounded by ignorant people in most jobs. I am ignorant a lot of times on my job, but I am aware of my ignorance, and I always try to correct my mistakes and improve.

When dealing with ignorant coworkers, do not respond, do not get angry, do not argue, and do not become ignorant yourself. You are not being paid to argue and prove a point. You are being paid to perform a job and make money for yourself and the company.

THINKING SKILLS 15

1. Out of every 100 prisoners in America, how many are high school dropouts?

_____

2. On average, how much more per year do high school graduates earn compared to students who dropped out?

_____

3. Why is it important to stay in school?

_____

_____

_____

_____

4. How do you prove to an employer that you have a commitment and willingness to work?

_____

_____

_____

_____

THINKING SKILLS 16

Write the words that each of the following represents.

1. 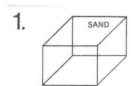 SAND

2. MAN
   BOARD

3. STAND
   I

4. |R|E|A|D|I|N|G|

5. WEAR
   LONG

6. R
   ROAD
   A
   D

7. T
   O
   W
   N
   V

8. CYCLE
   CYCLE
   CYCLE

9. LE
   VEL

10. O
    M. D
    B. A.
    PH. D

11. KNEE
    LIGHT

12. i i
    o o
    o o
    o o
    o o

13. CHAIR

14. (dice)

15. T
    O
    U
    C
    H
    V

16. GROUND
    (footprints)

17. MIND
    MATTER

18. HE'S / HIMSELF

19. ECNALG

20. DEATH   LIFE

1._____ 2._____ 3._____
4._____ 5._____
6._____ 7._____ 8._____
9._____ 10._____
11._____ 12._____
13._____ 14._____ 15._____
16._____ 17._____
18._____ 19._____
20._____

LETTERS FROM PRISON

T.A.E.
Serving 65 years for murder

A man without education is a walking fool. Education is a major source of enlightenment. Once I was able to get over my fear of not being able to read, and began reading at a college level, I am amazed at how open my mind has become. I began to learn and accept truth, and I now stand for something. An ignorant man is a blind man and is no good to mankind.

I always thought education was for nerds and boring people. I spent the better part of my high school years chasing women and having sex. History, English, and science never meant a thing to me on the streets while hustling or working dead-end jobs. The streets were my education. What I learned was good for survival on the streets. But what I learned got me to where I am now.

A convict gave me my first real book to read, *Destruction of Black Civilization*, and a dictionary. He told me to learn about myself and where I came from. Shortly afterward, I was able to enroll in college courses through the prison system. I found out that I was actually able to have informative and enlightening conversations. I now realize the importance of a good education.

FEAR TO MAKE A MISTAKE
James L. Adams

Fear to make a mistake, to fail, or to take a risk is perhaps the most general and common emotional block. Most of us have grown up rewarded when we produce the "right" answer and punished if we make a mistake. When we fail we are made to realize that we have let ourselves and others down. Similarly we are taught to live safely and avoid risk whenever possible. Obviously, when you try something new, whether it is a new job or improving your reading skill, you are taking a risk: of making a mistake, failing, feeling like a fool, getting your feelings hurt, or whatever.

This type of fear is to a certain extent realistic. Something new is usually a threat to the status quo, and is therefore resisted with appropriate pressure upon the person.

One of the better ways of overcoming such a block is to realistically assess the possible negative consequences of your new adventure.

THINKING SKILLS 17

1. When you do not understand something, what are three negative consequences of asking a question?

A. _____

B. _____

C. _____

2. When you do not understand something, what are three positive consequences of asking a question?

A. _____

B. _____

C. _____

3. Finish the following sentence:
   Without education, you're_____

   _____

FEAR IS AN ILLUSION
Michael Jordan

I never looked at the consequences of missing a big shot. Why? Because when you think about the consequences you always think of a negative result.

If I'm going to jump into a pool of water, even though I can't swim, I'm thinking about being able to swim at least enough to survive. I'm not jumping in thinking to myself, "I think I can swim, but maybe I'll drown." If I'm jumping into any situation, I'm thinking I'm going to be successful. I'm not thinking what happens if I fail.

But I can see how some people get frozen by that fear of failure. They get it from peers or from just thinking about the possibility of a negative result. They might be afraid of looking bad or being embarrassed.

I realized that if I was going to achieve anything in life I had to be aggressive. I had to get out there and go for it. I don't believe you can achieve anything by being passive. I know fear is an obstacle for some people, but it's an illusion to me.

Once I'm in there, I'm not thinking about anything except what I'm trying to accomplish. Any fear is an illusion. You think something is standing in your way, but nothing is really there. What is there is an opportunity to do your best and gain some success.

If it turns out my best isn't good enough, then at least I'll never be able to look back and say I was too afraid to try. Failure always made me try harder the next time.

That's why my advice has always been to "think positive" and find fuel in any failure. Sometimes failure actually just gets you closer to where you want to be. If I'm trying to fix a car, every time I try something that doesn't work, I'm getting closer to finding the answer. The greatest inventions in the world had hundreds of failures before the answers were found.

I think fear sometimes comes from a lack of focus or concentration. If I had stood at the free-throw line and thought about 10 million people watching me on the other side of the camera lens, I couldn't have made anything.

So I mentally tried to put myself in a familiar place. I thought about all those times I shot free throws in practice and went through the same motion, the same technique that I had used thousands of times. You forget about the outcome. You know you are doing the right things. So you relax and perform. After that you can't control anything anyway. It's out of your hands, so don't worry about it.

I approached practices the same way I approached games. You can't turn it on and off like a faucet. I couldn't dog it during practice and then, when I needed the extra push late in the game, expect it to be there.

But that's how a lot of people approach things. And that's why a lot of people fail. They say all the right things, make all the proper appearances. But when it comes right down to it, they're looking for reasons instead of answers.

If you're trying to achieve something, there will be roadblocks. I've had them; everybody has had them. But obstacles don't have to stop you. If you run into a wall, don't turn around and give up. Figure out how to climb it, go through it, or work around it.

Excerpts from pp. 8–11, 14–16 (580 words) from *I CAN'T ACCEPT NOT TRYING* by MICHAEL JORDAN and PHOTOGRAPHS BY SANDRO MILLER.
Copyrighted © 1994 by Rare Air, Ltd. Text © 1994 Michael Jordan. Photographs © 1994 by Sandra Miller.
Reprinted with permission from HarperCollins Publishers.

THINKING SKILLS 18

1. While playing basketball, why did Michael Jordan never think about the consequences of missing a big shot?

_____

_____

2. What did Michael Jordan think about while shooting a free throw?

_____

_____

_____

_____

3. What should you do when you have obstacles in your life?

_____

_____

_____

_____

SECTION 1

PERSONAL QUALITIES AND WORK ETHIC

SECTION 1
PERSONAL QUALITIES AND WORK ETHIC

FACTS ABOUT WORK

1. Employers are in business to make money and do not expect to babysit employees. Employers hire and retain people who are a solution to a problem and are not a problem themselves.
2. To remain employed, you must be able to control your emotions. Anger and violence are not problem-solving techniques, but a sign of an immature employee.
3. A new job will create a new set of problems for you.
4. You have to establish your own performance standards. An employee must add value to a position and be productive on bad and mad days. You must want more from a job than just a paycheck.
5. Any job is a good job and provides you with an opportunity to move on to a better position. You have to do first things first.
6. There is constant change on a job. Be prepared to deal with it.
7. Almost any job will become boring. There will be things you won't like about your job. Accept and adjust. If you have to complain, complain for positive results.
8. You must have a commitment and willingness to work: the ability to do what you don't feel like doing and doing it with a positive attitude. This requires self-discipline.
9. You must be willing to improve and develop your talents.
10. To become successful on a job, finish what you start, believe in yourself, and don't give up.

> 1. Employers are in business to make money and do not expect to babysit employees. Employers hire and retain people who are a solution to a problem and are not a problem themselves.

EMPLOYEES WHO NEED A BABYSITTER:

- Think anger and violence are problem-solving techniques
- Cannot control their emotions or language
- Are loud and disruptive
- Are not dependable or trustworthy
- Display the same behavior on a job that they display on the streets
- Resent authority
- Are not mature enough to follow rules
- Cannot forego immediate pleasures
- Complain all the time
- Bring their personal problems to work and take their frustrations out on fellow employees
- Have neglected their education
- Take everything personally
- Lack initiative
- Do not take pride in their work
- Do not have personal goals
- Do not care about quality work
- Give in to the temptation of stealing
- Do not think in terms of teamwork
- Lack a positive attitude

WITHIN THE FREEDOM TO CHOOSE
Stephen R. Covey

Within the freedom to choose are those endowments that make us uniquely human. In addition to *self-awareness,* we have *imagination*—the ability to create in our minds beyond our present reality. We have *conscience*—a deep inner awareness of right and wrong, of the principles that govern our behavior, and a sense of the degree to which our thoughts and actions are in harmony with them. And we have *independent will*—the ability to act based on our self-awareness, free of all other influences.

Even the most intelligent animals have none of these endowments. To use a computer metaphor, they are programmed by instinct and/or training. They can be trained to be responsible, but they can't take responsibility for that training; in other words, they can't direct it. They can't change the programming. They're not even aware of it.

But because of our unique human endowments, we can write new programs for ourselves totally apart from our instincts and training. This is why an animal's capacity is relatively limited and man's is unlimited. But if we live like animals, out of our own instincts and conditioning and conditions, out of our collective memory, we too will be limited.

> *EMPLOYERS HIRE AND RETAIN PEOPLE WHO ARE SOLUTIONS TO PROBLEMS AND NOT PROBLEMS THEMSELVES.*
>
> —Unknown Author

MORE AND MORE EMPLOYEES
Daniel Goleman

More and more employers are complaining about the lack of social skills in new hires. In the words of an executive at a large restaurant chain: "Too many young people can't take criticism—they get defensive or hostile when people give them feedback on how they're doing. They react to performance feedback as though it were a personal attack."

THINKING SKILLS 19

1. What does it mean to forego immediate pleasures?

_____

_____

_____

2. What does it mean to take something personally?

_____

_____

_____

3. Why is it not a good idea to bring your personal problems to work?

_____

_____

_____

4. List five personal qualities you must display on every job.

A._____

B._____

C._____

D._____

E._____

THINKING SKILLS 20

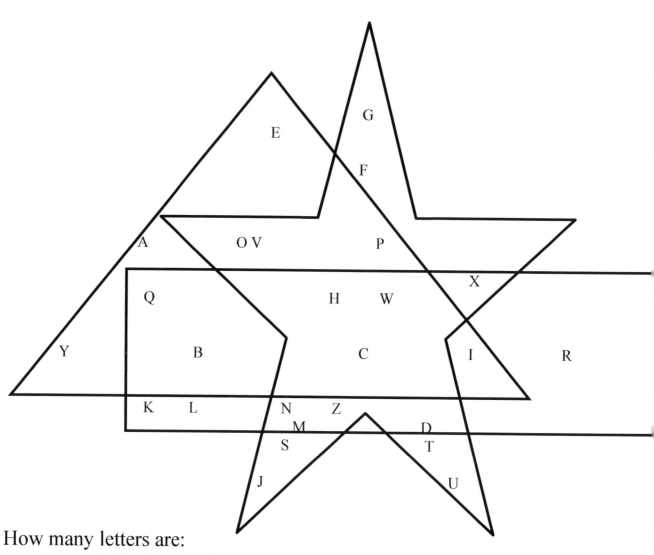

How many letters are:

_____1. In the star, but not in the triangle or rectangle?

_____2. In the triangle, but not in the star or rectangle?

_____3. In the rectangle, but not in the star or triangle?

_____4. Common to the star and rectangle, but not to the triangle?

_____5. Common to the triangle and rectangle, but not to the star?

_____6. Common to the star and triangle, but not to the rectangle?

Personal qualities are your personal characteristics.
Personal qualities make up your personality.

10 BASIC PERSONAL QUALITIES YOU MUST DISPLAY ON EVERY JOB:

1. Dependability
2. Discipline
3. Honesty
4. Maturity
5. Calm under pressure: control your emotions
6. Have the ability to get along with other employees
7. Excellent communication skills
8. Conscientious and helpful
9. Work ethic based on hard work
10. Have the ability to do things without being told

FOREGOING IMMEDIATE PLEASURES

There Can Be No Progress

There can be no progress, no achievement, without sacrifice, and a man's worldly success will be in the measure that he sacrifices his confused animal thoughts, and fixes his mind on the development of his plans, and the strengthening of his resolution and self-reliance. And the higher he lifts his thoughts, the more manly, upright, and righteous he becomes, the greater will be his success, the more blessed and enduring will be his achievements.

As A Man Thinketh,, James Allen (1864-1912), Dover Publications, Inc.

EMPLOYMENT NOTES

There is a limit to how much you can earn on any job. No matter how good a worker you are, your pay rate will top out. This is a major reason why you should always learn as much as you can about your job, learn new skills, strive to do your best, and display excellent soft skills. A good reference from your employer is priceless when applying for a new job.

When I finally allowed myself to face fully my own responsibility for my life, I began to grow. I began to change. And my self-esteem began to rise.

THINKING SKILLS 21

There was a young man who I worked with that was dependable, was an excellent worker, had an excellent attitude, and took initiative to do extra work. I mentioned to him that if he wanted to advance, he needed to be more mindful of his language and his playful behavior. He displayed the same playful behavior at work that he displayed outside of work.

He was eventually fired by the company for smoking pot during work. I also learned that he had just gotten out of jail before being employed by our company. Now, not only will he have trouble getting another job because of his incarceration, but he also has to overcome the mark against him of being fired from a job for drug use. It is too bad that he did not think in terms of consequences by foregoing his immediate pleasures.

1. What was this employee not able to do?

_____

2. What are three consequences of his choice?
   A._____
   B._____
   C._____

3. What would the positive consequences have been if he were able to forego his immediate pleasures?
   A._____
   B._____
   C. _____

4. List two reasons why he would have trouble getting another job.
   A. _____
   B._____

> 2. To remain employed, you must be able to control your emotions. Anger and violence are not problem-solving techniques, but are a sign of an immature employee.

EMOTIONAL COMMON SENSE
Rolland S. Parker

Most people are self-destructive. They behave in ways that are obviously against their best interest. They hurt themselves even though they know better. You the reader are probably self-destructive. Can you really assert that there is nothing that you have done yesterday or today that is not in your best interest? Would it be a safe bet that you just obtained a momentary satisfaction from an action that is against your preferred style of life or goals or values? Perhaps you have antagonized somebody or neglected to build up an important relationship.

Self-destructiveness means creating circumstances that ruin relationships, reduce creativity, permit others to take advantage, or continue harmful contacts with others in the name of "family" or "friendship" or "security." Self-destructiveness means not listening to others' needs and messages, thus enduring conflict and disappointment. Self-destructiveness means seeing oneself as valueless, becoming the target of someone's irrational anger, the patsy of the exploitative grasper, or the self-selected wallflower of life.

Self-destructiveness is also remaining unaware of one's own needs for support, for love, for self-assertion. It is laziness that demands immediate satisfaction as opposed to the long-range discipline of accomplishment.

The road . . . to the ultimate self-destructiveness is lined with hopelessness. The road to emotional common sense, to productivity, to happiness, to self-esteem is paved with self-understanding, optimism, and a useful goal.

THINKING SKILLS 22

1. List five examples of how employees can be self-destructive while at work.

A. _____

_____

B. _____

_____

C. _____

_____

D. _____

_____

E. _____

_____

2. Finish the following sentences:

A. The road to emotional common sense, to productivity,_____

_____

_____

_____

_____

B. It is laziness that demands_____

_____

_____

3. What is a self-destructive habit you may have?

_____

_____

_____

THINKING SKILLS 23

Snowflake Inspector #51 is on the lookout for any snowflake whose six sections do not match perfectly. The inspector will approve only two of these flakes. Can you find them and spot the mistakes in the other five?

All six sections match in snowflakes_____ & _____

VISUALIZE: SEEING THINGS IN THE MIND'S EYE
Visualize means to form a mental image of something that is not visible.

Victor Frankl
Stephen R. Covey

Victor Frankl was imprisoned in the death camps of Nazi Germany, where he experienced things that were so repugnant to our sense of decency that we shudder to even repeat them.

His parents, his brother, and his wife died in the camps or were sent to the gas ovens. Except for his sister, his entire family perished. Frankl himself suffered torture and countless dishonor, never knowing from one moment to the next if his path would lead to the ovens or if he would be among the "saved" who would remove the bodies or shovel out the ashes of those so fated.

One day, naked and alone in a small room, he began to become aware of what he later called "the last of the human freedoms" the freedom his Nazi captors could not take away. They could control his entire environment, they could do what they wanted to his body, but Victor Frankl himself was a self-aware being who could look as an observer at his very involvement. His basic identity was intact. **He could decide within himself how all of this was going to affect him.** Between what happened to him, or the stimulus, and his response to it, was his freedom or power to choose that response.

In the midst of his experiences, Frankl would project himself into different circumstances, such as lecturing to his students after his release from the death camps. He would describe himself in the classroom, in his mind's eye, and give his students the lessons he was learning during his very torture.

Through a series of such disciplines—mental, emotional, and moral, principally using memory and imagination—he exercised his small, embryonic freedom until it grew larger and larger, until he had more freedom than his Nazi captors. They had more **liberty**, more options to choose from in their environment; but he had more **freedom**, more internal power to exercise his options. He became an inspiration to those around him, even to some of the guards. He helped others find meaning in their suffering and dignity in their prison existence.

In the midst of the most degrading circumstances imaginable, Frankl used the human endowment of self-awareness to discover a fundamental principle about the nature of man: **Between stimulus and response, man has the freedom to choose.**

THINKING SKILLS 24

1. What do Michael Jordan and Victor Frankl have in common?

_____

2. How did Michael Jordan visualize and how did it help him?

_____

_____

_____

_____

_____

_____

3. How did Victor Frankl visualize and how did it help him?

_____

_____

_____

_____

_____

_____

4. Give an example of how visualization can help you.

_____

_____

_____

_____

CAN A PERSON MAKE YOU MAD OR ANGRY?

The answer to this question is no. A person cannot make you mad or angry. A person can be the stimulus, but you create your own response. When you get mad or angry, you are choosing that response. **"Between stimulus and response, man has the freedom to choose."** If a person can make you mad or angry, then you are being controlled by the other person.

A lot of employees react with their emotions and not with their minds. When things do not go their way on a job, they react before they think. If you feel yourself getting upset, a good technique is to visualize in your mind something you are trying to achieve or something pleasant. This will give you time to settle down and help in choosing a positive response to whatever is upsetting you. A negative response with an outburst of emotions will usually get you suspended or fired.

It is not uncommon to get yelled at by a supervisor on a job. The supervisors and manager are under a lot of pressure from their bosses. You have to train yourself not to respond in a negative manner. Victor Frankl did it while being tortured; you can certainly do it on a job when something unpleasant happens to you. The next time you get angry, visualize what you are trying to accomplish or a pleasant moment in your life.

The undisciplined mind is like an elephant. If left to blunder around out of control, it will wreak havoc. But the harm and suffering we encounter as a result of failing to restrain the negative impulses of mind far exceed the damage a rampaging elephant can cause. Not only are these impulses capable of bringing about the destruction of things, they can also be the cause of lasting pain the others and to ourselves.

THINKING SKILLS 25

1. Close your eyes and visualize yourself leaving your house in the morning.

2. Close your eyes and visualize looking down at this class from the upper right-hand front corner of the room.

3. With your eyes open, visualize yourself having a good time with your friends or family.

4. Close your eyes and visualize bacon cooking on the stove and smelling the bacon.

5. Close your eyes and visualize yourself brushing your teeth and tasting the toothpaste.

6. With your eyes open, visualize what you are going to accomplish in the next five years.

EMPLOYMENT NOTES

The level of visualization that Victor Frankl and Michael Jordan used takes a lot of concentration and practice. But like anything else, the more you practice, the easier it becomes. When having problems at work, visualize what you are trying to accomplish through your job rather than getting upset and reacting. Focus on something positive.

Visualization is just the process of thinking of something good or an enjoyable moment in a bad situation. A good time to visualize is when you feel yourself becoming angry. It can help to save your job and your future.

TO BECOME EMOTIONAL
S. A. Swami, Ph.D.

To become emotional is human. It is the very spice of living. Yet, emotions must be handled with care. Anger, fear and grief are the negative emotions which have the potential to ruin the life of any person, if he or she gives in to them. Even the positive emotion of joy needs to be kept within bounds. When emotion takes over the mind, the intellect and its power of reasoning are pushed overboard, with the result that the person's decisions and actions no longer reflect his or her best interest in the long run.

Spontaneous display of anger is harmful to your mental health. It can ruin friendships and interpersonal relationships. But, learning to manage anger is a step towards self-excellence. Such a learning calls for a self-analysis as to why you get angry in the first place. Though the arousal of anger is a complex psycho-neurological phenomenon not fully understood yet, psychologists have traced it to the "value-system" or "sense of values" of the person.

When an event in the world is viewed by the person as a threat to his survival or as a conflict to his or her personal sense of values and expectations, the emotion of anger is triggered. Anger management calls for a few extra moments of deliberate reflection on the event, rather than a spontaneous explosion of word or deed. The few moments of secondary thinking will help in broadening the perspective of the event, and also provide an opportunity for a calculated alternate course of response to the event.

There is nothing wrong in a verbal expression of anger so long as it does not trigger a conflict in the value-system of the other person. How you say it is as important as what you say. But, the key is in your immediate return to a state of composure and calmness.

Anger management is possible only when you develop a healthy sense of respect for the other person as a human being who has as much right for his or her personal sense of values as you have for yours. Anger creates more problems than it can solve. For this reason the wise consider that to be able to control and transcend anger in life is the greatest of all virtues.

SELF-EXCELLENCE: KEY TO PREVENTIVE STRESS MANAGEMENT & GOAL ORIENTED LIVING, by S. A. Swami, Ph.D., Published by Minibook Publishing Co. Reprinted with permission from Mrs. Swami.

MISGUIDED ANGER ONLY CAUSES PROBLEMS

How many times have you witnessed someone trying to solve his or her problems by becoming angry or violent? A lot of people use anger and violence as a problem-solving technique. They have never matured enough to realize that anger and violence can only cause more problems. You cannot solve any problems when you become angry and violent.

EXPLOSIVE TEMPERS

How many people do we know who sour their lives, who ruin all that is sweet and beautiful by explosive tempers, who destroy their poise of character and make bad blood! It is a question whether the great majority of people ruin their lives and mar their happiness by lack of self-control. How few people we meet in life who are well balanced, who have that exquisite poise which is characteristic of the finished character.

As A Man Thinketh, by James Allen (1864-1912), Dover Publications, Inc.

EXPOSURE TO VIOLENCE

Children exposed to adult violence, particularly interfamilial adult violence (between family members), may learn from these adults that aggressive behavior is a viable problem-solving option, and that physical aggression in close relationships is normal. Clearly, such lessons could create problems for children on the playground and later in life.

Researchers have observed that exposure to violence is related to difficulties regulating anger, frustration, and other negative feelings, as well as deficits in understanding and experiencing empathy for the feelings of others. These difficulties can lead to significant behavioral and social problems for children. As noted above, one way in which children deal with overwhelming negative feelings is through behavioral distraction. Performance in academic settings will suffer if violence-exposed children attempt to cope with anger towards other children or frustration with academic material by behaving disruptively. Moreover, children with deficits in emotion regulation, empathy, and understanding emotions tend to be rated as less popular and more rejected by their peers.

Education Encyclopedia – StateUniverslty.com

QUOTES FOR DISCUSSION

Whatever is begun in anger ends in shame.

—Ben Franklin (1706–1790)

How much more grievous are the consequences of anger than the causes of it.

—Marcus Aurelius (121 AD–180 AD)

Holding on to anger is like grasping a hot coal with the intent of throwing it at someone else; you are the one who gets burned.

—Buddha (563 BC–483 BC)

Speak when you are angry and you will make the best speech you will ever regret.

—Ambrose Bierce (1842–1913)

It's not what happens to you, but how you react to it that matters.

—Epictetus (55 AD–135 AD)

If evil be spoken of you and it be true, correct yourself, if it be a lie, laugh at it.

—Epictetus (55 AD–135 AD)

Anger will never disappear so long as thoughts of resentment are cherished in the mind. Anger will disappear just as soon as thoughts of resentment are forgotten.

—Buddha (563 BC–483 BC)

Reject your sense of injury and the injury itself disappears.

—Marcus Aurelius (121 AD–180 AD)

Anger: an acid that can do more harm to the vessel in which it is stored than to anything on which it is poured.

—Mark Twain (1835–1910)

Anger is like those ruins which smash themselves on what they fall.

The deferring of anger is the best antidote to anger.

The greatest remedy for anger is delay.

—Seneca (4 BC–65 AD)

Anger, if not restrained, is frequently more hurtful to us than the injury that provokes it.

It is often better not to see an insult than to avenge it.

—Seneca (4 BC–65 AD)

Do not do to others what angers you if done to you by others.

—Socrates (469 BC–399 BC)

I will permit no man to narrow and degrade my soul by making me hate him.

—Booker T. Washington (1856–1915)

One minute of patience can result in ten years of peace.

—Italian proverb

Life is a tragedy for those who feel, and a comedy for those who think.

—La Bruyere

If you are patient in one moment of anger, you will escape a hundred days of sorrow.

Once you pour the water out of the bucket it's hard to get it back in it.

—Chinese proverb

For every minute you remain angry, you give up sixty seconds of peace of mind.

—Ralph Waldo Emerson (1803–1882)

When anger rises, think of the consequences.
Before you embark on a journey of revenge, dig two graves.

—Confucius (551 BC–479 BC)

Anger dwells only in the bosom of fools.

—Albert Einstein (1879–1955)

I was angered, for I had no shoes. Then I met a man who had no feet. —Chinese proverb

THINKING SKILLS 26

Count the number of squares.

How many squares do you see?_____

THE COMPLETE THINKER: A HANDBOOK OF TECHNIQUES FOR CREATIVE AND CRITICAL PROBLEM SOLVING, by Barry F. Anderson, copyright © 1980 by Prentice-Hall Inc. Published by Prentice-Hall, Inc. Reprinted with permission from Barry F. Anderson.

WHY DO PEOPLE FIGHT?

- Low self-esteem
- Immaturity
- Lack of goals
- Lack of self-confidence
- No problem-solving skills
- Out of touch with what is important in life
- Have been deeply hurt and never dealt with it
- Emotionally unstable
- Have not developed the ability to think in terms of consequences
- Do not have any values
- No self-control
- Peer pressure
- Act before they think
- Fear what other people will think of them if they walk away from a fight
- Lack emotional skills, cognitive skills, and behavioral skills

EMPLOYMENT NOTES

It is very shocking how many employees get in physical fights while at work. Even if you win, you lose. You will lose your job and it will be very difficult to get another job. You also lose any type of good recommendation from the employer. A major trait employers look for when hiring is the ability to control your emotional, cognitive, and behavioral skills

EMOTIONAL SKILLS

- Identifying and labeling feelings
- Expressing feelings
- Assessing the intensity of feelings
- Managing feelings
- Delaying gratification
- Controlling impulses
- Reducing stress
- Knowing the difference between feelings and actions

COGNITIVE SKILLS

- Self-talk—conducting an "inner dialogue" as a way to cope with a topic or challenge or reinforce one's own behavior
- Reading and interpreting social cues—for example, recognizing social influences on behavior and seeing oneself in the perspective of the larger community
- Using steps for problem-solving and decision-making—for instance, controlling impulses, setting goals, identifying alternative actions, anticipating consequences
- Understanding the perspective of others
- Understanding behavioral norms (what is and is not acceptable behavior)
- A positive attitude towards life
- Self-awareness—for example, developing realistic expectations about oneself

BEHAVIORAL SKILLS

- Nonverbal—communicating through eye contact, facial expressions, tone of voice, gestures, and so on.
- Verbal—making clear request, responding effectively to criticism, resisting negative influences, listening to others, helping others, participating in positive peer groups.

W. T. Grant Consortium on the School-Based Promotion of Social Competence, "Drug and Alcohol Prevention Curricula," in J. David Hawkins et al, *Communities That Care* (San Francisco: Jossey-Bass, 1992), Reprinted with permission from John Wiley & Sons, Inc.

WHAT PART OF MY LIFE?

1. What part of my life is it that I am unhappy with? What part of my character or my behavior displeases me?
2. Am I expecting someone else to solve the problem for me? Or am I prepared to accept responsibility for myself and for changing myself?
3. What can I do to change? What am I doing now that I should stop? What am I doing that I should start doing?

When you have answered these questions you have arrived at the required state of self-knowledge. You may well have experienced your own Flash of Insight. You are ready to break down the problem into bite-size pieces that you can handle. Awareness will lead to motivation. You are now getting ready to send your negative emotional habits packing.

From *WHEN AM I GOING TO BE HAPPY? HOW TO BREAK THE EMOTIONAL BAD HABITS THAT MAKE YOU MISERABLE*, by Penelope Russianoff and Joseph E. Persico, copyright © 1988 by Penelope Russianoff and Joseph E. Persico. Reprinted with permission from Bantam Books, a division of Random House, Inc.

Seeing who I really am, it is silly to ever feel basically inadequate, because anything I really need to do, I have the necessary resources for. There is no need to be fearful of the future; I now see that death, trouble, and pain are not evils which one must be resigned to, but, rather experiences which contribute to human growth. Whereas I may have once thought that people could hurt my feelings, or make me angry, resentful or bitter, or cause me embarrassment, I now see that in a very real sense no one can hurt me unless I let them.

—William W. Harman

THIS MAY SHOCK YOU
Charles Swindoll

This may shock you, but I believe the single most significant decision I can make on a day-to-day basis is my choice of attitude. It is more important than my past, my education, my bankroll, my successes or failures, fame or pain, what other people think of me, or say about me, my circumstances, or my position. The attitude I choose keeps me going or cripples my progress. It alone fuels my fire or assaults my hope. When my attitudes are right, there's no barrier too high, no valley too deep, no dream too extreme, no challenge too great for me.

Yet we must admit that we spend more of our time concentrating and fretting over the things that can't be changed than we do giving attention to the one that we can changed, our choice of attitude. Stop and think about some of the things that suck up our attention and energy, all of them inescapable: the weather, the wind, people's action and criticisms, who won or lost the game, delays at airports or waiting rooms, x-ray results, gas and food costs.

Quit wasting energy fighting the inescapable and turn your energy to keeping the right attitude. Those things we can't do anything about shouldn't even come up in our minds; the alternative is ulcers, cancer, sourness, depression.

Let's choose each day and every day to keep an attitude of faith and joy and belief and compassion.

Take charge of your own mind!

COUNT TO TEN
Neil Eskelin

For years, psychology gurus have recommended blowing off steam when you're angry—as long as no one is harmed. We've been told that hitting a punching bag or throwing our fist into a pillow will help alleviate the tension.

Well, new research indicates that the opposite effect may occur. Your quick-release steam valve may actually increase your anger.

In a study conducted by psychologists from Iowa State University and Case Western Reserve, 700 college students who were insulted by an unseen partner were placed in a situation where they could direct a blast of noise at the person they believe insulted them.

The control group tried to let off steam by hitting a punching bag for two minutes. It didn't matter. In fact, their responses became even more angry. The findings were reported in the Journal of Personality and Social Psychology.

I am convinced the best way to reduce anger is to take a few deep breaths, count to ten, and let negative feelings dissipate slowly. Blowing your top—even if no one hears you—is tough on your nervous system.

THINKING SKILLS 27

1. Define "self-talk."

_____

_____

_____

2. Explain how you can use self-talk to overcome a difficult challenge.

_____

_____

_____

_____

_____

_____

3. List six emotional skills.

A._____

B._____

C._____

D._____

E._____

F._____

4. Define "verbal skills."

_____

_____

_____

_____

3.   A new job will create a new set of problems for you.

- Temporary surrender of security
- Transportation
- Child care
- Uniform or clothing expense
- Problems with supervisors
- Getting yelled at by a supervisor
- Problems with other employees
- Problems with customers
- Having to work under pressure and stress
- Not liking the job or type of work
- Poor working conditions
- Work schedule
- Lacking soft skills
- Being assigned harder jobs than others
- Lazy coworkers
- Not being recognized for working hard
- Low pay
- Having to sacrifice family events and personal life because of work
- Feeling of being looked down upon
- Being assigned more work than coworkers
- Being blamed by a supervisor for other workers' mistakes
- Being unjustly accused by a coworker
- Not being given the proper instructions on how to accomplish a task
- Criticism from others
- Incompetent managers
- Having to work overtime when you already have plans
- Hard and tiring work
- Not being able to take breaks
- Not having proper equipment
- Incorrect paycheck
- Working outside in all types of weather
- Other employees making more money
- Employee gossip
- Family problems outside of work

THINKING SKILLS 28

List some problems you might experience on a job and how you will handle the problems if they arise. (If you are already working, list problems that you experienced when you started your job.)

1. _____

_____

2. _____

_____

3. _____

_____

4. _____

_____

5. _____

_____

TEMPORARY SURRENDER OF SECURITY

Security comes from being in control, being in a comfortable environment with your friends, and being in an environment where you know what you should do and how to act. You will not have this security when you walk into a business for your first day of work. The first week on a job is usually the hardest. A new job is a learning experience and every day will get easier. If you come across a work situation in which you do not know what to do, ask a supervisor. All the other employees around you experienced this same surrender of security when they started, even if they will not admit it.

THINKING SKILLS 29

ST. IVES

As I was going to St. Ives, I met a man with seven wives, Each wife had seven sacks, each sack had seven cats, Each cat had seven kits: kits, cats, sacks, and wives. How many were going to St. Ives?

THE COMPLETE THINKER: A HANDBOOK OF TECHNIQUES FOR CREATIVE AND CRITICAL PROBLEM SOLVING, by Barry F. Anderson, copyright © 1980 by Prentice-Hall Inc. Published by Prentice-Hall, Inc. Reprinted with permission from Barry F. Anderson.

Answer:_____

QUOTES FOR DISCUSSION

None of us can be free of conflict and woe. Even the greatest men have had to accept disappointments as their daily bread.

—Bernard M. Baruch (1870–1965)

Man is fond of counting his troubles, but he does not count his joys. If he counted them up as he ought to, he would see that every lot has enough happiness provided for it.

—Fyodor Dostoevsky (1821–1881)

The two most powerful warriors are patience and time.

—Leo Tolstoy (1828–1910)

Work spares us from three evils: boredom, vice, and need.

—Voltaire (1694–1778)

If you neglect your work, you will dislike it; if you do it well, you'll enjoy it.

—Sir Philip Sidney (1554–1586)

Out of difficulties grow miracles.

—Jean de la Bruyere (1645–1696)

We are born weak, we need strength; helpless, we need aid; foolish, we need reason. All that we lack at birth, all that we need when we come to man's estate, is the gift of education.

—Jean Jacques Rousseau (1712–1778)

When you're finished changing, you're finished.

—Benjamin Franklin (1706–1790)

Strong character is brought out by change, weak ones by permanence.

—Jean Paul (1763–1825)

They must change who would be constant in happiness and wisdom.

—Confucius (551 BC–479 BC)

The reward of suffering is experience.

—Aristophanes (450 BC–385 BC)

NEW TASKS OF DEVELOPMENT

1. Having self-discipline

2. Having self-confidence

3. Not giving up when faced with a challenge

4. Willing to change

5. Willing to forego immediate pleasures

6. Controlling your emotions

7. Accepting responsibility for your own life

8. Realizing life is not easy

9. Not comparing yourself to others

10. Maintaining a positive attitude

If

By Rudyard Kipling (1865–1936)

If you can keep your head when all about you
Are losing theirs and blaming it on you,
If you can trust yourself when all men doubt you
But make allowance for their doubting too,
If you can wait and not be tired by waiting,
Or being lied about, don't deal in lies,
Or being hated, don't give way to hating,
And yet don't look too good, nor talk too wise:

If you can dream—and not make dreams your master,
If you can think—and not make thoughts your aim;
If you can meet with Triumph and Disaster
And treat those two impostors just the same;
If you can bear to hear the truth you've spoken
Twisted by knaves to make a trap for fools,
Or watch the things you gave your life to, broken,
And stoop and build 'em up with worn-out tools:

If you can make one heap of all your winnings
And risk it on one turn of pitch-and-toss,
And lose, and start again at your beginnings
And never breathe a word about your loss;
If you can force your heart and nerve and sinew
To serve your turn long after they are gone,
And so hold on when there is nothing in you
Except the Will which says to them: "Hold on!"

If you can talk with crowds and keep your virtue,
Or walk with kings—nor lose the common touch,
If neither foes nor loving friends can hurt you;
If all men count with you, but none too much,
If you can fill the unforgiving minute
With sixty seconds' worth of distance run,
Yours is the Earth and everything that's in it,
And—which is more—you'll be a Man, my son!

IT'S NOT WHAT HAPPENS TO US

Stephen R. Covey

It's not what happens to us, but our response to what happens to us that hurts us. Of course, things can hurt us physically or economically and can cause sorrow. But our character, our basic identity, does not have to be hurt at all. In fact, our most difficult experiences become the crucibles that forego our character and develop the internal powers, the freedom to handle difficult circumstances in the future and to inspire others to do so as well.

IF CONRAD FERDINAND MEYER HAD DIED
Thomas Armstrong

If Conrad Ferdinand Meyer had died at the age of forty, he would hardly have been missed. As a child and student he had been restless, lead astray, and moody. As an adult he wandered from job to job without focus or direction. At the age of twenty-seven he entered a mental institution where he suffered from hypochondria and the delusion that "all people found him disgusting." He came close to putting an end to his life.

Then at forty, everything changed. As Ernst Kretschmer, author of *The Psychology of Men of Genius,* wrote: "Until his fortieth year he appeared stunted and lean as a skeleton, and only at this age did his beard begin to grow and his figure to take on the later fullness and stateliness. And at this age for the first time appeared a collection of poems." He continued to write for the next twenty-seven years and became one of Switzerland's most beloved poets.

Meyer's poetic genius is remarkable for its sudden appearance. But in a larger sense his story shows us how an ability can remain hidden for years· like an underground stream and burst forth unexpectedly as a fountain of vitality. We all have potential like Meyer's waiting for the opportunity to express itself. Each of us possesses hidden intelligences that lie dormant like seeds in winter, waiting for the spring to blossom.

4. You have to establish your own performance standards. An employee must add value to a position and be productive on bad and mad days. You must want more from a job than just a paycheck.

- If all the employees worked exactly the same, there would be no reason to promote anyone.
- If your performance standards were just like all the other employees, there would be no pay raises.
- Remain focused and do the best job you can.
- Long-term employees will sometimes put pressure on you not to perform better than they perform.
- Be mature enough not to let job peer pressure interfere with your long-term career goals.
- It is easier and more satisfying to be a hard worker than a person who hardly works.
- You get paid for doing a good job, so do the job correctly.
- If your objective is to advance, you will want to be more productive than the other employees.
- You will always have job-related setbacks; correct them and move on.
- Perform to your best even when you do not feel like it.
- Honesty is a huge part of your work performance.
- You have to take the road less traveled.

THE ROAD NOT TAKEN
Robert Frost

Two roads diverged in a yellow wood
And sorry I could not travel both
And be one traveler, long I stood
And looked down one as far as I could
To where it bent in the undergrowth

Then took the other as just as fair
And having perhaps the better claim
Because it was grassy and wanted wear
Though as for that, the passing there
Had worn them really about the same

And both that morning equally lay
In leaves no step had trodden black
Oh, I kept the first for another day!
Yet, knowing how way leads onto way
I doubted if I should ever come back

I shall be telling this with a sigh
Somewhere ages and ages hence
Two roads diverged in a wood
And I took the one less traveled by
And that has made all the difference

THINKING SKILLS 30

1. What comparisons can be made to "The Road Not Taken" and your work performance? Give an example.

_____

_____

_____

_____

_____

_____

2. List five reasons why you should establish your own performance standards.

A. _____

B. _____

C. _____

D. _____

E. _____

EMPLOYMENT NOTES

If you cannot resist stealing from an employer because you want to be an honest person, resist stealing because of the cost involved when you get caught. Take your per hour rate times the number of hours you work per week. Multiply this number by at least 36 weeks. Employers are very careful not to hire people who steal, so it will take some time before you get another job. Add in your legal costs. A lot of employers are starting to prosecute employees who get caught stealing. Is stealing worth it?

SETTING YOUR OWN PERFORMANCE STANDARDS

"The Road Less Traveled" exemplifies an important life skill and work-related trait—that is, to set your own performance standards and to not follow the crowd. Entry-level employees starting a new job are usually not aware of work expectations or company expectations. A lot of companies do not have a good work orientation to inform new employees of their job duties and roles within the company. The only clue the new employee has is to watch how other employees perform the job. On-the-job training is usually based on following and learning from a current employee.

Observe, listen, and learn. Base your performance standards on expectations set by the company and not on poor recommendations of other employees. Listen and follow the rules set by your boss or supervisor, and do not listen to other employees on how to get around the rules. New employees who set their own performance standards often are labeled as "favorites" by other employees. The best way to deal with this is to not let it affect you. Focus on your long-term plan. If other employees make negative comments to you, do not react in a negative manner. This is what they want. Just smile and make a joke about it. If you react in a negative manner to the comments, they will keep doing it. If you ignore the comments, eventually the comments will not matter to you and the person making the comments will have no reason to continue. This will be a major step in developing your leadership skills.

THE PRINCIPLE OF SOCIAL PROOF
Robert B. Cialdini

This principle states that we determine what is correct by finding out what other people think is correct. The principle applies especially to the way we decide what constitutes correct behavior. *We view a behavior as correct in a given situation to the degree that we see others performing it.* Whether the question is what to do with an empty popcorn box in a movie theater, how fast to drive on a certain stretch of highway, or how to eat the chicken at a dinner party, the actions of those around us will be important guides in defining the answer.

The tendency to see an action as appropriate when others are doing it works quite well normally. As a rule, we will make fewer mistakes by acting in accord with social evidence than by acting contrary to it. Usually, when a lot of people are doing something, it is the right thing to do. This feature of the principle of social proof is simultaneously its major strength and its major weakness. Like the other weapons of influence, it provides a convenient shortcut for determining the way to behave but, at the same time, makes one who uses the shortcut vulnerable.

EMPLOYMENT NOTES

New employees are very vulnerable to the bad habits of older employees. If a new employee sees a long-term employee sitting down or hiding, the new employee usually follows along. If a new employee sees a long-term employee breaking a rule, the new employee will usually break the same rule. This is why you have to establish your own performance standards based on the company's policies and not on the habits of other employees.

EMPLOYMENT NOTES

Getting noticed at work for positive reasons will get you ahead.
Getting noticed at work for negative reasons will get you fired.

THINKING SKILLS 31

Each question consists of a series of five symbols on the left half of the page. Next to these are five other symbols labeled A, B, C, D, and E. Study the first five symbols to determine what is happening in the series. Then select the one lettered symbol that best continues the series.

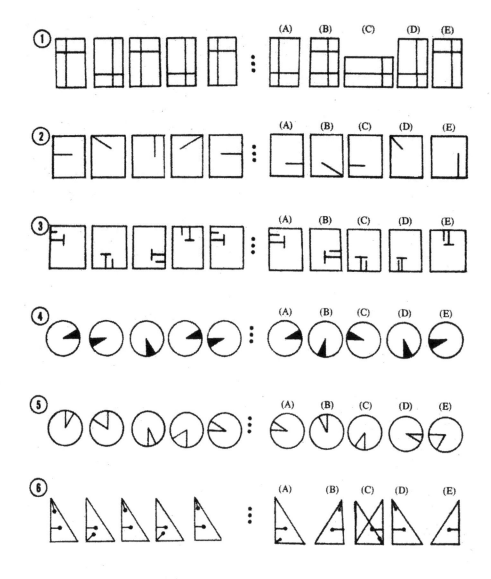

From *Peterson's Mechanical Aptitude and Spatial Relations Tests,* 6th Edition. Copyright 2004. Reprinted with permission from Peterson's, a Nelnet company.

JOB SUCCESS

In order to be successful on a job, employees have to care how other people view them because they are judged by their behavior. Any negative behavior displayed outside of work should not be displayed during work. Employees must be professional with customers, coworkers, bosses, and vendors on every job. Displaying positive behavioral traits while at work will increase your chances for a pay raise, promotion, and continued employment.

You will be judged by your actions. Loud and disruptive behavior, playful behavior, and profane language are the most common downfalls of most entry-level workers. It is usually just a bad habit to talk loud or to always use curse words. This may not offend you, but it does offend other people. It indicates to your boss that you lack self-discipline and the ability to control yourself. A basic job trait is to be considerate of others. Using loud and profane language is not being considerate of others. This sends a message to others around you that you are inconsiderate. Do not waste you hard work. Have people view you as you really are—an excellent worker and a person who cares about being employed.

THINKING SKILLS 32

IF YOU WERE THE BOSS?

If you were a boss, which individual attributes do you think a person displays who is loud, disruptive, and constantly curses in front of strangers?

Displays self-control	versus	Lacks self-control
Thinks in terms of consequences	versus	Does not care about consequences
Focuses on job	versus	Does not focus on job
Cares about job	versus	Does not care about job
Shows respects for others	versus	Lacks respect for others
Educated	versus	Uneducated
Wants to advance	versus	Does not want to advance
Understands company policy	versus	Refuses to adjust
Professional	versus	Unprofessional
Displays soft skills	versus	Lacks soft skills

EMPLOYMENT NOTES

When a company has to lay off workers, a deciding factor in who gets laid off and who remains on the job is a combination of the above attributes. Make sure you display the proper job attributes.

INITIATIVE

Doing something above and beyond your job-related responsibilities

Helping other people without being told

Seeing an activity through to completion

Not having to be instructed every day on what needs to be done and when to start

Not having to be supervised

Cleaning your work area without being instructed

Discovering better ways to perform your job

Solving work-related problems to help the company increase profits

Helping new employees adjust to the job

EMPLOYMENT NOTES

When you see something that needs to be done and it is outside of your job description, it does not hurt to just do the extra work. Initiative is a building block to being successful on a job.

THINKING SKILLS 33

1. List five examples of how you have displayed initiative in your daily life.

A. _____

_____

B. _____

_____

C. _____

_____

D. _____

_____

E. _____

_____

2. Why is it important to take initiative at work?

_____

_____

_____

3. What are two major benefits you can get from taking initiative at work?

A. _____

B. _____

THE GOLDEN EAGLE
Anthony de Mello

A man found an eagle's egg and put it in a nest of a barnyard hen. The eagle hatched with the brood of chicks and grew-up with them. All his life, the eagle did what the barnyard chicks did, thinking he was a barnyard chicken. He scratched the earth for worms and insects. He clucked and crackled. And he would thrash his wings and fly a few feet in the air.

Years passed and the eagle grew very old. One day he saw a magnificent bird above him in the cloudless sky. It glided in graceful majesty among powerful wind currents, with scarcely a beat of its strong golden wings.

The old eagle looked up in awe. "Who's that?" he asked.

"That's the eagle, the king of the birds," said his neighbor. "He belongs to the sky. We belong to the earth—we're chickens." So the eagle lived and died a chicken, for that's what he thought he was.

THINKING SKILLS 34

1. Define the term "performance standards."

_____

_____

_____

_____

2. What does "The Golden Eagle" have to do with setting your own performance standards?

_____

_____

_____

_____

3. Explain what the following Plato quote has to do with performance standards: "People are like dirt. They can nourish you and help you grow as a person or they can stunt your growth and make you wilt and die."

_____

_____

_____

_____

QUOTES FOR DISCUSSION

Man is manacled only by himself: thought and action are the jailers of Fate—they imprison; thought and action are also the angels of Freedom—they liberate.

—James Allen (1864–1912)

The circumstances which a person encounters with suffering are the result of his or her mental in-harmony. The circumstances which a person encounters with blessedness are the result of his or her mental harmony.

—James Allen (1864–1912)

The aphorism, "As a person thinks in his or her heart, so is he or she," not only embraces the whole of a person's being, but is so comprehensive as to reach out to every condition and circumstance of life. A person is literally what he or she thinks, and the person's character being the complete sum of all of his or her thoughts.

As a plant springs from the seed and could not be without, so every act of man springs from the hidden seeds of thought, and could not have appeared without them.

—James Allen (1864–1912)

The greatest discovery of any generation is that human beings can alter their lives by altering the attitudes of their minds.

—William James (1842–1910)

Each man is the architect of his own fate.

—Appius Claudius (340 BC–272 BC)

Choose a job you love, and you will never have to work a day in your life.

—Confucius (551 BC–479 BC)

5.   Any job is a good job and provides you with an opportunity to move on to a better position. You have to do first things first.

There is no future in any job. The future lies in the person who holds the job.

—Dr. George W. Crane (1901–1995)

Nothing great is created suddenly, any more than a bunch of grapes or a fig. If you tell me that you desire a fig, I answer you that there must be a time. Let it first blossom then bear fruit, then ripen.
First say to yourself what would you be; and then do what you have to do.

—Epictetus (55 AD–135 AD)

RIGHT PRINCIPLES
James Allen

It is wise to know what comes first, and what to do first. To begin anything in the middle or at the end is to make a mess of it. The athlete who began by breaking the tape would not receive the prize. He must begin by facing the starter and toeing the mark, and even then a good start is important if he is to win. The pupil does not begin with algebra and literature, but with counting and ABC. So in life, the businessmen who begin at the bottom achieve the more enduring success.

The first things in a sound life, and therefore in a truly happy and successful life, are *right principles.* Without right principles to begin with, there will be wrong practices to follow with, and a bungled and wretched life to end with. All the infinite variety of calculations which tabulate the commerce and science of the world, come out of the ten figures; all the hundreds of thousands of books which constitute the literature of the world, and perpetuate its thought and genius, are built up from the twenty-six letters. The greatest astronomer cannot ignore the ten simple figures. The wisest of men cannot dispense with the twenty-six simple characters. The fundamentals in all things are few and simple; yet without them there is no knowledge and no achievement. The fundamentals, the basic principles in life or true living, are also few and simple, and to learn them thoroughly, and study how to apply them to all the details of life, is to avoid confusion, and to secure a substantial foundation.

Foundation Stones To Happiness And Success, by James Allen, Cosimo Classics, originally published in 1913,

THE FIVE PRINCIPLES ARE FIVE PRACTICES, FIVE AVENUES TO ACHIEVE, AND FIVE SOURCES OF KNOWLEDGE
James Allen

1. Duty

Undivided attention to the matter at hand, intelligent concentration of the mind on the work to be done; it includes all that is meant by thoroughness, exactness, and efficiency.

2. Honesty

It involves the absence of all cheating, lying, and deception by word, look, or gesture. It includes sincerity, the saying what you mean, and the meaning what you say.

3. Economy

The conservation of one's financial resources is merely the beginning leading toward the more spacious chambers of true economy. It means the wise use of one's physical ability and mental resources.

4. Generosity

The giving of money is the smallest part of generosity. There is the giving of thoughts, and deeds, and sympathy, the bestowing of goodwill, and being generous towards your opponents.

5. Self-control

Its neglect is the cause of vast misery, innumerable failures, and tens of thousands of financial, physical, and mental wrecks. The lessons of patience, purity, gentleness, kindness, and firm loyalty are contained in the principle of self-control, are slowly learned by men, yet until they are truly learned, a man's character and success are uncertain and insecure.

Foundation Stones To Happiness And Success, by James Allen, Cosimo Classics, originally published in 1913

THINKING SKILLS 35

1. What does "undivided attention to the matter at hand" mean?_____

_____

_____

2. How do you wisely use your physical ability and mental resources? _____

_____

_____

_____

3. How can you bestow goodwill?_____

_____

_____

4. Describe a kind act you have performed within the last week._____

_____

_____

_____

THINKING SKILLS 36

1. Three men checked into a hotel room. The manager told them that the price of the room was $30. Each man paid $10, and they went up to their room. Later, the manger discovered that the price of their room was really $25, so he sent the bellboy to return $5 to them. The bellboy, who was nobody's fool, realized that the $5 could not be split three ways evenly, so he kept $2 and gave the men back $3. Thus each of the three men got back $1 of his $10 and hence paid $9.

Now, three times $9 equals $27, and this plus the bellboy's $2 equals $29. What happened to the other dollar?

_____

_____

_____

_____

2. Do First Things First:

If you only had one match and you entered a room to start a kerosene lamp, an oil heater, and a wood stove, which would you light first?

— *Author Unknown, Source Unknown*

Explain:_____

_____

_____

Question 1: *THE COMPLETE THINKER: A HANDBOOK OF TECHNIQUES FOR CREATIVE AND CRITICAL PROBLEM SOLVING*, by Barry F. Anderson, copyright © 1980 by Prentice-Hall Inc. Published by Prentice-Hall, Inc. Reprinted with permission from Barry F. Anderson.

FIRST THINGS FIRST

1. Get a good education and continue to learn.

2. Establish a stable work history.
   - Do not job hop. Employers look down upon people who move from one job to another. Every entry-level job can help you demonstrate your ability to commit yourself to a job and help you create a stable employment history.

3. Strive to get a good recommendation from your current employer.
   - When leaving a job, get a written recommendation from your current employer. The only way to accomplish this is to follow all company rules, be dependable and trustworthy, and display excellent soft skills.
   - When applying for a new job, the new employer will usually call your previous employers to find out about your past job performance.
   - Never burn bridges. It can hurt you in the future.
   - If you have to quit a job before you have another job, always give at least a two weeks' notice.
   - Never quit and walk off a job.

4. Do not expect to be paid a high wage for an entry-level position.
   - Employers pay high wages for employees who can offer them something in return. With no previous experience or training, what do you have to offer an employer? The answer to this can be an excellent attitude, well-developed soft skills, and eventually a good job recommendation from a previous employer.

5. Develop a positive attitude.
   - Expect work-related problems and don't respond in a negative manner.
   - Do not take constructive criticism personally.
   - Focus on your soft skills.
   - Be more productive than anyone else.
   - Do not mind what other employees say about you.
   - Do not respond to negative comments.
   - Set obtainable goals.

QUOTES FOR DISCUSSION

The three great essentials to achieve anything worthwhile are, first, hard work; second, stick-to-itiveness; third, common sense.

—Thomas Edison (1847–1931)

The successful person makes a habit of doing what the failing person doesn't like to do.

—Thomas Edison (1847–1931)

Start by doing what is necessary; then do what's possible; and suddenly you are doing the impossible.

—St. Francis of Assisi (1181–1226)

By failing to prepare, you are preparing to fail.

—Benjamin Franklin (1705–1790)

What we are is what we have thought for years.

—Gautama the Buddha (560-480 BC)

I find that the harder I work, the more luck I seem to have.

—Thomas Jefferson (1801–1890)

One of the prevailing sources of misery and crime is in the generally accepted assumption that because things have been wrong a long time, it is impossible they will ever be right.

—John Ruskin (1819–1900)

While we are making up our minds as to when we shall begin, the opportunity is lost.

—Marcus Fabius Quintilian (35 AD–95 AD)

Many receive advice, only the wise profit from it.

—Publilius Syrus (first century BC)

Opportunity is missed by most people because it is dressed in overalls and looks like work.

—Thomas Edison (1847–1931)

Folks who never do any more than they are paid for, never get paid more than they do.

—Elbert Hubbard (1856–1915)

THINKING SKILLS 37

1. Define the phrase "to burn bridges on a job."

_____

_____

_____

2. List five ways in which you can "burn bridges" on a job.

A. _____

B. _____

C. _____

D. _____

E. _____

3. List five ways in which you can control your own future on a job.

A. _____

B. _____

C. _____

D. _____

E. _____

THINKING SKILLS 38

1. If "too" is pronounced "too" and "two" is also pronounced "too," how should you spell and pronounce the second day of the week?

_____

2. What gets wetter as it dries?

_____

3. Five days before the day before yesterday is Wednesday. What day is three days from today?

_____

4. Rearrange the letters in the words "new door" to make one word.

_____

5. In a year there are 12 months; 7 months have 31 days. How many months have 28 days?

_____

WHY COMPANIES LOSE CUSTOMERS

Companies rise and fall in their customers' favor for a variety of reasons. The American Society for Quality Control reports the following study showing the relative importance of several reasons companies lose customers:

1%..........Die

3%..........Moved away

5% ....Influenced by friends

9%..........Lured away by the competition

14%........Dissatisfied with product

68%........Turned away by an attitude of indifference on the part of a company employee

Source: THE PRYOR REPORT, Vol. 10, No. 4a.
LESSONS FORM THE FIELD, by Howard Feiertag and John Logan

EMPLOYMENT NOTES

No matter how good it would feel to just quit and walk off of a job because something went wrong, don't do it. The long-term feeling of being unemployed is more intense and more hurtful than the short-term gratification of quitting. It also makes it harder to get another job. Always try to find another job before you quit, and give a notice.

> 6. There is constant change on a job. Be prepared to deal with it.

THINKING SKILLS 39

1. On the line below, write the word *attitude* with your usual writing hand.

_____

2. On the line below, write the word *attitude* with your other hand.

_____

When you look at the word *attitude* written by the hand you do not write with, you see a picture of the kind of attitude we usually have when trying to do something new or trying to do something we do not want to do.

Any "first-time" experience threatens our security. We feel awkward and incompetent, forcibly removed from our familiar "comfort zone."

LIFE WANTS US TO

Life wants us to grow, to expand, to take things to the next level, to evolve. And it has wired us accordingly. We are built for growth, expansion and evolution. Yet, growth means exchanging the old for the new—and we often find ourselves reluctant or unwilling to let go.

We procrastinate. We excuse. We postpone. We rationalize. We deny. We bargain. We "explain away." *We resist*. And life goes on as it was—without any change. As Walt Kelly once remarked, "We have met the enemy and he is us."

What's needed are ways to take ourselves out-of-the-mind to embody the changes we want to make. The stepping stones provide a clear path to follow.

Thoughts	➡	Words
Words	➡	Action
Actions	➡	Habits
Habits	➡	Character
Character	➡	Destiny

From the Internet website evolutionarypathways.com
Reprinted with permission.

EVERYTHING BEGINS WITH

Your life is what your thoughts make it.
—Marcus Aurelius

Everything begins with our thinking. Like a river, thoughts flow through our lives and give birth to everything we say and do.

Words are thoughts in tangible form. Words are thoughts "in formation"—or information. This information is crucial to our personal growth and self-development. It is no mistake that this is the first stepping stone of out-of-the-mind self-improvement and motivation.™

We use words to define our reality. We use them to describe who we are, what we want, and where we are going. We use them to define what is possible. The language we use delineates the boundaries of our thinking and of our world.

We first make our habits; and then our habits make us.
—John Dryden

Our actions and habits flow naturally from the way we think. They also condition our thinking. Actions and habits are the second stepping stone of out-of-the-mind self-improvement and motivation.™

From the Internet website evolutionarypathways.com
Reprinted with permission.

HARNESSING THE POWER

Harnessing the power of action & habit is to harness the power of everyday. Whatever falls into our daily routine gets done on a regular basis. Whatever doesn't usually gets postponed, rejected or ignored. We *become* what we do on a regular basis.

The power of everyday either works for us or it works against us—but it's always working. Sow on a daily basis and you *will* reap. Fail to sow on a daily basis and you may very well weep.

Tapping into the power of habit is one of the surest ways to take control of our lives.

Destiny is not a matter of chance, but a matter of choice. It is not a thing to be waited for; it is a thing to be achieved.

—William Jennings Bryant

There is a mysterious element to character and destiny. There *are* forces beyond our control which influence how our destiny unfolds. Yet, not everything is out of our hands.

We can change the way we think. We can consciously shape our habits. We can polish character.

Destiny is the fruition of a life. It's also a road we walk. When we walk *consciously* we bring the process of our life to a whole new level. We see that we can accept, change and evolve. Our path becomes an upward spiral of personal growth and fulfillment on so many levels.

From the Internet website evolutionarypathways.com
Reprinted with permission.

QUOTES FOR DISCUSSION

Life belongs to the living, and he who lives must be prepared for changes.

—Johann Wolfgang von Goethe (1749–1832)

I do not think much of a man who is not wiser today than he was yesterday.

—Abraham Lincoln (1809–1865)

The dogmas of the quiet past are inadequate to the stormy present. The occasion is piled high with difficulty, and we must rise with the occasion. As our case is new, so we must think anew and act anew.

—Abraham Lincoln (1809–1865)

Everyone thinks of changing the world, but no one thinks of changing himself.

—Leo Tolstoy (1828–1910)

It is not the strongest of the species that survive, nor the most intelligent, but the one most responsive to change.

—Charles Darwin (1809–1882)

Growth is the only evidence of life.

—John Henry Newman (1801–1890)

Without continual growth and progress, such words as improvement, achievement, and success have no meaning.

—Benjamin Franklin (1705–1790)

True life is lived when tiny changes occur.

—Leo Tolstoy (1828–1910)

Change in all things is sweet.

—Aristotle (384 BC–322 BC)

Have patience with all things, but chiefly have patience with yourself. Do not lose courage in considering your own imperfections but instantly set about remedying them—every day begin the task anew.

—Saint Francis de Sales (1567–1622)

They must often change, who would be constant in happiness or wisdom.

—Confucius (551 BC–479 BC)

PAPER WALLS

PRISON FROM THE CRADLE TO THE GRAVE
H. G. Wells

But when a man has once broken through the paper walls of everyday circumstance, those fragile walls that hold so many of us securely imprisoned from the cradle to the grave, he has made a discovery. If the world does not please you, you can change it. Determine to alter it at any price, and you can change it altogether. You may change it to something sinister and angry, to something appalling, or you may change it to something brighter, something more agreeable, and at the worst something much more interesting. There is only one sort of man who is absolutely to blame for his own misery. That man is the one who finds life dull and dreary. There are no circumstances in the world that determination cannot alter.

From *THE HISTORY OF MR. POLLY,* Published in 1910, H. G. Wells

WHAT ARE PAPER WALLS?

- Resisting change
- Not realizing that you have just as much talent as the next person
- Thinking that you never will be successful
- Not having confidence in yourself
- Giving up
- Being controlled by your emotions
- Fearing success
- Fearing failure
- Having a low opinion of yourself
- Thinking other people are smart and you are not
- Lacking basic reading and math skills
- Having ill-defined goals
- Lacking motivation
- Thinking life is easy
- Lacking self-discipline
- Not helping other people

THINKING SKILLS 40

1. What are some common changes you will have to deal with on a job?

A. _____

B. _____

C. _____

D. _____

E. _____

2. What are positive ways to deal with change?

A. _____

B. _____

C. _____

D. _____

E. _____

STANDARD CHANGES THAT OCCUR ON A JOB:

- New managers or supervisors
- Job assignments
- Rules and regulations
- Pay rates
- Job descriptions
- Benefits
- Altered job performance
- Ownership
- New employees
- Performance standards
- Work days and hours
- Dress codes
- Department transfer
- Layoffs
- Uniforms
- Increased workload
- Lunch hour and break times
- Performance reviews
- Responsibility and control
- Equipment (or lack of proper equipment)

CHANGE IN THE WORKPLACE

- Always expect change and be prepared to deal with it.
- Do not fear change. View it as an opportunity.
- Do not resist change in the workplace. Be positive and adapt quickly.
- Build a good working relationship with new managers. This gives you the opportunity to display your knowledge about your job.
- If your job duties increase and you have to do more work, be positive and accept your new responsibilities.
- Resisting change and complaining about it might make you feel better, but it will increase your chances of losing your job.
- You are being paid to do a job how the company wants it done, not how you want it done.

> 7. Almost any job will become boring. There will be things you won't like about your job. Accept and adjust. If you have to complain, complain for positive results.

- The working world is not a democracy.
- There will be things you won't like about your job.
- A lot of employers do not care about their employees, but they expect the employee to care about them. Do not let this affect your productivity.
- The main concern of a business is to make money.
- Focus on what you are trying to accomplish through your job. Do not focus on things that you disagree with or think are unfair.
- Always remember that managers and supervisors are not perfect and will make mistakes.
- If you are the best worker, more will be expected of you.
- If you are the best worker, you will usually be given the hardest job. Take it as a compliment.
- Work assignments are usually not fair.
- A lot of times it is not what you know but who you know. Strive to keep a good working relationship with your boss.
- There are a lot of lazy employees. Don't let this affect your productivity or attitude.

THERE ARE JOBS WHERE YOU COULD BE:

- The most deserving worker and not be the highest-paid employee
- The most knowledgeable worker and not be the person who is promoted
- The most productive worker and not get the best schedule
- The most dependable worker and not be appreciated
- The worker with the best attitude and still get yelled at by a supervisor
- The most honest worker and not be trusted
- The worker who takes the most initiative and still have a supervisor order you around even though you know what to do
- The hardest worker and get in trouble for taking a break
- The employee who is always solving work-related problems and the supervisor takes all the credit
- The employee with the most experience but given little credit for your experience
- The most responsible employee but given little responsibility

What word describes how you should handle the above situations?_____

THINKING SKILLS 41

1. List five traits that a mature person does not display on a job.

A. _____

_____

B. _____

_____

C. _____

_____

D. _____

_____

E. _____

_____

2. Finish the following statements.

There are jobs where you could be:

A. The most deserving worker and _____

_____

B. The most productive worker and _____

_____

C. The most dependable worker and _____

_____

D. The worker with the best attitude and _____

_____

E. The hardest worker and _____

_____

EMPLOYMENT NOTES

You might as well accept the fact that there could be times at work when you will not be treated fairly. The sooner you accept this, the more prepared you will be to deal with it. There will be other employees who are treated better than you and they will not deserve the treatment. They will receive higher pay, better job assignments, a better schedule, and more perks. A lot of times on a job it depends on who you know and not what you know.

The best way to deal with unfair treatment is to use it as motivation to outperform other employees and move up or on to a better position.

The worst way to deal with this is to develop a negative attitude toward your supervisors, constantly complain about it, or have it affect your productivity. Stay focused on what you are trying to accomplish.

THINKING SKILLS 42

1. This will confuse your mind and keep you trying over and over again to see if you can outsmart your foot, but you can't. It is preprogrammed in your brain!

   A. While sitting in a chair, lift your right foot off the floor and make clockwise circles.

   B. Now, while doing this, draw the number 6 in the air with your right hand. Your foot will change direction.

   —Author Unknown, Source Unknown

2. If you were to spell out each number (one, two, three, etc.), at what number would the letter "A" be part of the spelling?

_____

MAN IS MADE OR UNMADE BY HIMSELF

Man is made or unmade by himself. In the armory of thought he forges the weapons by which he destroys himself. He also fashions the tools with which he builds for himself heavenly mansions of joy and strength and peace. By the right choice and true application of thought, man ascends to the divine perfection. By the abuse and wrong application of thought he descends below the level of the beast. Between these two extremes are all the grades of character, and man is their maker and master.

As A Man Thinketh, James Allen (1864–1912), Dover Publications, Inc.

BIGGEST MISTAKE

The biggest mistake you can make in life is to think you work for somebody else! Yes, you may receive a paycheck where you work and you likely have a boss, but you are the only one in charge of your own work, job and career!

Author: Bob Nelson, PhD, *1001 WAYS TO REWARD EMPLOYEES, and 1001 WAYS TO TAKE INITIATIVE AT WORK.* www.drbobnelson.com. Reprinted with permission from Bob Nelson.

THE JOB
Anthony de Mello

First person applying for the job:
"You do understand that this is a simple test we are giving you before we offer you the job that you applied for?"
"Yes."
"Well, what is two plus two?"
"Four," said the applicant.

Second person applying for the job:
"Are you ready for the test?"
"Yes."
"Well, what is two plus two?"
"Whatever the boss says it is."

The second applicant got the job.

EMPLOYMENT NOTES

An employee has to perform his or her job according to how the boss wants the job performed, not according to how the employee thinks the job should be performed. Every company has work standards that all employees must follow. Do not listen to other employees; listen to your boss.

THINGS COULD ALWAYS BE WORSE
Anthony de Mello

"I am in desperate need of help—or I'll go crazy. We're living in a single room—my wife, my children, and my in-laws. So our nerves are on edge, we yell and scream at one another. The room is a hell."

"Do you promise to do whatever I tell you?" said the Master gravely.

"I swear I shall do anything."
"Very well. How many animals do you have?"
"A cow, a goat, and six chickens."
"Take them all into the room with you. Then come back after a week."

The disciple was horrified. But he had promised to obey! So he took the animals in. A week later he came back a helpless figure, moaning, "I'm a nervous wreck. The dirt! The stench! The noise! We're all on the verge of madness!"

"Go back," said the Master, "and put the animals out."

The man ran all the way home. When he came back the following day, his eyes were sparkling with joy. "How sweet life is! The animals are out. The home is a Paradise, so quiet and clean and roomy!"

HOW TO COMPLAIN FOR POSITIVE RESULTS
Michael C. Thomsett

Some people get into the habit of communicating their problems to someone else, expecting the other person to come up with a solution. They burn their bridges. They overlook what should be obvious: When you burn a bridge on one side, it becomes useless on the other side as well.

Taking a negative approach may be your first impulse, but it's an impulse worth resisting. Before expressing any idea to someone else, stop and think. How will it sound to the other person? Is the issue that person's problem, or is it yours? Would a team effort be the best approach to arriving at a solution? The rule of etiquette when you communicate a complaint to someone else is: Take responsibility for the solution, even if only as one of several participants. Try to avoid the assumption that your job is to bring a problem to someone else's attention and that the other person's job is to fix it.

When you take the negative approach, you also gain the reputation you most want to avoid. You become known as a complainer, rather than as an action-oriented problem solver. This attribute does not inspire others to work with you cooperatively, but forces them away…

Listen to your style of communication. Avoid negative statements. Come up with more positive ways to state your concerns. For example, consider these negative statements and the positive alternatives:

NEGATIVE	POSITIVE
I hate it when…	Wouldn't it be better if…
Why can't you…	What if we…
This is stupid…	What about this alternative…
This will never work out because…	I had another idea you might consider…

Expressing yourself in negative terms creates the impression in others that you see issues only in the most negative way. That does not lead to cooperation; it only causes other people to avoid working with you.

People also feel alienated from those who express themselves in absolute terms. If you find yourself falling into this habit, fight the impulse. It comes from wanting to emphasize your position but often produces an outcome that is the opposite of what you wish to achieve. For example, consider the following absolute statements and the alternatives:

ABSOLUTE	NONABSOLUTE
He always says…	I have heard him say…
Nothing ever gets done around here…	We have had our problems at times…
Everyone thinks…	Many people seem to think…
We must do it this way…	Here's a good idea to consider…

When you communicate in positive and nonabsolute terms, you receive the response you seek. Those who employ the diplomatic approach may complain just as much as others, but with this difference—people listen to them and are more likely to respond. For example, think about the people with whom you work. . . . You are probably more willing to respond when they communicate with you in positive, motivating terms. Those who come to you only with complaints that they expect you to solve elicit resistance or unwilling compliance.

THINKING SKILLS 43

1. Write a positive alternative to the following negative statements:

NEGATIVE	POSITIVE
I hate it when…	_____
Why can't you…	_____ _____
This is stupid…	_____ _____
This will never work out because…	_____ _____

2. Write a nonabsolute statement to the following absolute statements:

ABSOLUTE	NONABSOLUTE
He always says…	_____ _____
Nothing ever gets done around here…	_____ _____
Everyone thinks…	_____ _____
We must do it this way…	_____ _____

EMPLOYMENT NOTES

When working for a company, it is easy to find things to complain about. If complaining starts to become a habit, remind yourself that the company is providing you with a paycheck and there are a lot of people lined up to take your job. You have a choice to stop complaining so much or find another job. If you find another job, it will not be long before you find something to complain about. Be careful that your complaining does not interfere with your productivity or quality of work. I have done my share of complaining and it never helped anything.

> **8.** You must have a commitment and willingness to work: the ability to do what you don't feel like doing and doing it with a positive attitude. This requires self-discipline.

Willpower and Self-Discipline
Remez Sasson

Willpower is the ability to overcome laziness and procrastination. It is the ability to control or reject unnecessary or harmful impulses. It is the ability to arrive to a decision and follow it with perseverance until its successful accomplishment. It is the inner power that overcomes the desire to indulge in unnecessary and useless habits, and the inner strength that overcomes inner emotional and mental resistance for taking action. It is one of the corner stones of success, both spiritual and material.

Self-discipline is the companion of willpower. It endows with the stamina to persevere in whatever one does. It bestows the ability to withstand hardships and difficulties, whether physical, emotional or mental. It grants the ability to reject immediate satisfaction, in order to gain something better, but which requires effort and time.

Everyone has inner, unconscious, or partly conscious impulses; making them say or do things they later regret saying or doing. On many occasions people do not think before they talk or act. By developing these two powers, one becomes conscious of the inner, subconscious impulses, and gains the ability to reject them when they are not for his/her own good.

These two powers help us to choose our behavior and reactions, instead of being ruled by them. Their possession won't make life dull or boring. On the contrary, you will feel more powerful, in charge of yourself and your surroundings, happy and satisfied.

Author: Remez Sasson. From the website: www.SuccessConsciousness.com. Reprinted with permission from Remez Sasson

WHAT IS SELF-DISCIPLINE?

It is the ability to perform your job and be productive when:

- You are tired
- You do not feel well
- You are angry
- You have family problems
- You have to work harder than other employees
- You know you are getting paid less than other employees
- You get yelled at by a supervisor
- You are short of help
- You are under pressure
- You are under stress
- You do not have the proper equipment
- You have poor working conditions
- You are too hot or too cold
- You wanted to go to a party with your friends but are scheduled to work
- You requested a day off and it was denied
- You do not like your job
- You feel unappreciated
- Your coworkers are lazy
- Another employee is trying to start a confrontation with you and you do not respond
- Other employees are making fun of you because the boss likes the way you work hard
- Other employees are pressuring you to be just as lazy as them

DISCIPLINE
Laurence G. Boldt

Discipline is simply a matter of doing what we must, without wasting time or energy worrying about whether or not we feel like it. When we develop the habit of plunging in without whining, complaining, or procrastinating, we are on our way to genuine freedom.

We may not want to face it in such stark terms, but the choice is self-discipline or dependency; boss yourself or be bossed. We require a boss because we lack the discipline to boss ourselves. We resent the boss because he or she reminds us of our dependency. Resentment, in turn, robs us of the creative power we need to break the yoke of dependency. As we break through the comfort zones of limited thinking and habitual behavior, we discover that freedom is not the ability to do what we feel like doing but the ability to choose what to do and follow through.

From *ZEN SOUP* by Laurence G. Boldt, copyright © 1997 by Laurence G. Boldt. Reprinted with permission from Penguin, a division of Penguin Group (USA) Inc.

EMPLOYMENT NOTES

It takes more energy to try to figure out ways to do less work and to get out of work than it does to just apply yourself and do more work than you are paid for. Time goes by much faster.

THINKING SKILLS 44

1. Define self-discipline.

_____

_____

_____

_____

2. In what ways can you improve your self-discipline?

A. _____

B. _____

C. _____

D. _____

E. _____

_____

THINKING SKILLS 45

1. Write down eight words that are spelled the same forward and backward.

   A. _____

   B. _____

   C. _____

   D. _____

   E. _____

   F. _____

   G. _____

   H. _____

2. Four days from now is Sunday. What is the first day from today that contains the letter "N"?

   _____

3. What letter is next in this sequence? _____

   O, T, T, F, F, S, S, E…

4. Today is Monday. What day is six days after the day after tomorrow?

   _____

QUOTES FOR DISCUSSION

He who cannot obey himself will be commanded.
This is the nature of living creatures.

—Friedrich Nietzsche (1844–1900)

What it lies in our power to do, it lies in our power not to do.

—Aristotle (384 BC–322 BC)

He who reins within himself and rules passions, desires, and fears is more than a king.

—John Milton (1608–1674)

To enjoy freedom we have to control ourselves.

—Virginia Woolf (1882–1941)

He who lives without discipline dies without honor.

—Icelandic proverb

Hold yourself responsible for a higher standard than anybody else expects of you. Never excuse yourself. Never pity yourself. Be a hard master to yourself—and be lenient to everybody else.

No man is such a conqueror, as the one that has defeated himself.

—Henry Ward Beecher (1813–1887)

Your own mind is a sacred enclosure into which nothing harmful can enter except by your promotion.

—Ralph Waldo Emerson (1803–1882)

Rule your mind or it will rule you.

—Horace (65 BC–8 BC)

No evil propensity of the human heart is so powerful that it may not be subdued by discipline.

—Seneca (4 BC–65 BC)

Man must be disciplined, for he is by nature raw and wild.

—Immanuel Kant (1724–1804)

Where one person shapes their life by precept and example, there are a thousand who have shaped it by impulse and circumstances.

—James Russell Lowell (1819–1891)

TIPS TO IMPROVE YOUR SELF-DISCIPLINE

1. Make a to-do list of what you want to accomplish each day. Start small.

2. Even if you do not feel like it, accomplish your to-do list on a daily basis.

3. Think. Do not let your feelings control you.

4. Stay focused on finishing what you start.

5. Don't get discouraged. Give yourself positive feedback even when you don't accomplish everything you want.

6. Do something productive every day. Make it a habit.

For a man to conquer himself is the first and noblest of all victories.

—Plato (428 BC–348 BC)

Surveys show that 73% of all workers are less motivated today than they used to be, and 84% could perform significantly better if they wanted to. Perhaps most shocking of all, a full 50% of workers say they are exerting only enough energy to hang on to their jobs!

EMPLOYMENT NOTES

Your success at any job will depend on your self-discipline. It includes the ability to understand the consequences behind the choices you make concerning work. If you are always late, then you are not leaving early enough. If you are tired, then you are not getting enough rest. If your attitude is poor, then you are not doing enough to improve your self-talk. If any of the above keeps happening, then you will not be on the job very long.

ATTITUDES

Charles Swindoll

The longer I live, the more I realize the impact of attitude on life.

Attitude to me is more important than facts.

It is more important than the past,

Than education, than money,

Than circumstances, than failures, than successes,

Than what other people think or say or do.

It is more important than appearance, giftedness, or skill.

It will make or break a company.

It will cause a church to soar or sink.

It will be the difference in a happy home or a home of horror.

The remarkable thing is you have a choice every day regarding the attitude you will embrace for that day.

We cannot change our past.

We cannot change the fact that people will act a certain way.

We cannot change the inevitable.

The only thing we can do is play on the one string we have, and that is our attitude.

I am convinced that life is 10 percent what happens to me and 90 percent how I react to it.

And so it is with you.

PRISONER OF NEGATIVITY
Bonnie Moss

Make not your thoughts your prison.

—Antony and Cleopatra

Negativity is a prison with no walls to see, to feel or to touch. It is a prison with no visible, no physically confining barrier that hides the world outside.

Negativity can be a formidable and unforgiving jailer. You feel the strong shackles that bind you; you are in perpetual blindfold, unable to see any light. There is no day or night, you feel confined in the darkness, at times weighted down with the heaviness of condemnation from a cold and cruel world that has singled you out as its victim!

Negativity is a jailer with no mercy. It shows no compassion, deaf to reason and has no faith in the possibility of redemption.

Negativity wants to keep you in prison for as long as possible. It wields enough energy and power to keep you in bondage.

BUT—you hold the key to your freedom!

How did you get there?

Negativity demands a lot of energy!

Energy is wasted and comes with crippling effects mentally, emotionally, physically and spiritually. Negativity obscures the chances for happiness and a chance at a fulfilling life.

Problems have many faces and tend to visit almost everyone. There are many who are lost in their problems and forget there is a bigger world outside the problems. No problem lasts forever.

Negative thoughts end up in self-sabotage. Some common faces of negativity:
- Focus on what's missing or lacking

- Feelings of being unlucky
- Constantly putting yourself down
- Acceptance of failure as part of your fate
- Blaming the world and everyone else
- Victim mentality—the world is out to get you
- Unable to appreciate the blessings around you
- Unable to take action in order to find fulfillment
- Wallow in misery, constant complaining
- Negative self-image that you project to the world
- Negative attitude, low energy, loss of focus
  and motivation
- Unable to see or grab opportunities
- Unable to see what is good in the world
- Unhappy, miserable and prone to stress ailments
- Unhealthy lifestyle, suffers bouts of depression
- Unsuccessful relationships
- Moves more easily in a like world of negativity

Chart your course to freedom

No amount of therapy or pep talk can help unless you are ready and willing to set yourself free. Then, seek the help of supportive family members, friends and professional advice. You have to take that first step and acknowledge that there is a better way. No one can push you to it.

You alone can open the door to freedom, to a wonderful free world with lots of possibilities with a positive attitude.

Paint your world with the colors of brightness, joy, peace and love.

PRISONER OF NEGATIVITY by Bonnie Moss, Ezine Articles. Her website, http://goldencupcafe.tripod.com. Reprinted with permission from Bonnie Moss.

ONE OF THE SUREST CLUES

Dr. Penelope Russianoff

One of the surest clues that you have become hooked on negative thinking is if you are continually asking yourself, "What will people think?" That phrase is a red warning flag. If you find yourself asking it often, if the opinions of others dictate how you behave, beware. You are on dangerous ground. The phrase is almost always an indicator of faulty thinking. And erroneous thinking lies at the heart of most emotional bad habits.

- Guilt: "What will people think if I leave my child and take a job?"
- Fear of rejection: "What will that gorgeous guy think if I try to start a conversation with him?"
- Low self-esteem: "What will my friends think if I try to get out of their blue-collar world?"
- Self-flagellation: "What will the boss think when he finds out I lost the contract?"

In each case, the red flag is flying. It is warning us that we are thinking incorrectly. It is tipping us off to an emotional bad habit. Rather than asking, "What will people think?" we should be asking, "What do I think? What is right for me? What do I want for myself?"

From *WHEN AM I GOING TO BE HAPPY? HOW TO BREAK THE EMOTIONAL BAD HABITS THAT MAKE YOU MISERABLE*, by Penelope Russianoff and Joseph E. Persico, copyright © 1988 by Penelope Russianoff and Joseph E. Persico. Reprinted with permission from Bantam Books, a division of Random House, Inc.

9.	You must be willing to improve and develop your talents.

THE PROCESS OF REMOVING OBSTACLES
Thomas Armstrong

The process of removing obstacles to growth can be as simple as forgoing certain daily habits. Researchers estimate, for example, that roughly half of American adults leisure time is spent in front of a television set. Over a period of forty years, that represents tens of thousands of hours that could more profitably be spent learning a foreign language, practicing a musical instrument, developing a new business idea, building crafts project, or engaging hundreds of other activities. By simply choosing to refrain or reducing activities that do virtually nothing to move you into exploring new intellectual terrain, you can open windows of time to pursue the development of your hidden potentials.

Sometimes, the obstacles to realizing one's potential are more damaging. Drugs, alcohol, and other addictions are particularly poisonous to the awakening of talents and abilities. In such cases it may be imperative that a person get out of an unhealthy environment before he or she can find space to grow. Motivational speaker Og Mandino tells the story of how he had reached the end of his rope at the age of thirty-five. A failure in his work life, divorced, and alcoholic, he spent much of his time in bars. One rainy night he contemplated buying a gun and ending it all but instead sought refuge in a local library. The quiet in the library provided him with the opportunity to think clearly for the first time in years. It also exposed him to books, especially books on philosophy and self-esteem, which he began to devour over the next few months. This led to his discovery of his real talents as a salesman and motivational expert. His book *The Greatest Salesman in the World* has sold several million copies, and his speaking talents are sought after throughout the world. For other people, recovery groups, psychotherapy, or other forms of renewal may be instrumental in getting them out of negative patterns of feeling, thinking, and behaving that stand in the way of their becoming who they really are.

From *7 KINDS OF SMART, REVISED & UPDATED EDITION* by Thomas Armstrong, copyright © 1993, 1999 by Thomas Armstrong. Reprinted with permission from Plume, an imprint of Penguin Group (USA) Inc.

THINKING SKILLS 46

1. What habits do you have that could be considered obstacles to your growth?

A. _____

_____

B. _____

_____

C. _____

_____

D. _____

_____

E. _____

_____

2. How do you plan to change these habits?

_____

_____

_____

_____

_____

BREAKING BAD HABITS: 5 SIMPLE STEPS FOR CHANGING A HABIT
T. McDonald

"Good habits are hard to develop but easy to live with," and "Bad habits are easy to develop but hard to live with," according to Brian Tracey, a well-known motivational teacher. You may recognize that to successfully manage habit changes, breaking bad habits may be required in order to develop new ones.

Breaking bad habits takes at least 21 days. Of course, in difficult cases, it can take as long as a year. Here's an example of the process of how to change an unhealthy habit to a healthy habit. Suppose you've decided that coffee is not good for you and right now, you drink coffee with sugar daily. The new habit you would like to institute is to drink herbal tea without sugar.

At first, it may be challenging to break the bad habit of drinking coffee. You will have to use self-discipline for the first few weeks but gradually it will get easier. Once you are able to change the old habit to a new healthier one, it will serve you very well. Habits are remarkable because they don't require thinking. You just "do it" for years until you find yourself changing the habit again.

Here are 5 easy steps for changing habits:

1. **Awareness:** You must become aware of your habits. What is this habit exactly? How is this bad habit or group of bad habits affecting you? How is this habit affecting others? For example, smoking often has negative effects on others as well as on you.

2. **Wanting to Change:** As someone with a health problem, you must decide that breaking bad habits through a conscious effort is a worthy goal. You must convince yourself that the change in the habit is worth the effort involved.

3. **Commitment:** You must be determined to do whatever it takes for breaking bad habits so that you can better control your life. You make a decision that "no matter what" you will change the habit. You do the work required to stop. Here are some examples of habits you might want to change: Smoking, eating too much, eating processed foods, not exercising, drinking coffee or other beverages with caffeine in them, eating too much sugar or fat, drinking alcohol, procrastinating, etc.

4. **Consistent Action:** It is important to focus on changing just one habit at a time. Then, take consistent daily actions for breaking the bad habit that has been causing problems and take the actions to develop a new one. We suggest doing this process one step at a time rather than trying to do it all at once. Sometimes changing a habit can be done "cold turkey" like smoking and sometimes it works better to make a gradual change.

Be sure to give yourself positive rewards often for taking small actions toward changing a bad habit. Continual day-by-day actions are what are critical. This is NOT about an occasional action or step. It is about being consistent every day.

5. **Perseverance:** There will be times when you question whether it is all worth it. You'll say to yourself that breaking these bad habits is too difficult; that you are too "weak" to change. Your old self, often so comfortable living with the bad habits, is trying to hold on. Breaking your old patterns may require meditation and prayer.

Visualize regularly the rewards for following through and the costs of not following through on breaking the bad habits and especially the value to your future of building new better habits.

Get support from others, especially other people who want to make changes in their lives and read about people who have been successful in breaking bad habits. Affirm that, no matter what, you will not backslide into your old bad habit patterns.

Now, you are armed with a 5-step process for breaking any bad habit or other condition that requires changing. If you have an addiction to something such as alcohol, these steps alone may not be enough. You may require additional professional help or a support group, but for most cases this 5-step process will do the trick!

T. McDonald is a lifelong student of inner growth and a writer. She writes and edits several websites, including http://www.diabetes-guide.org and http://www.success77.com. Reprinted with permission from T. McDonald

THE 7 HABITS OF HIGHLY EFFECTIVE PEOPLE
Stephen R. Covey

1. BE PROACTIVE

2. BEGIN WITH THE END IN MIND

3. PUT FIRST THINGS FIRST

4. THINK WIN/WIN

5. SEEK FIRST TO UNDERSTAND, THEN TO BE UNDERSTOOD

6. SYNERGIZE

7. SHARPEN THE SAW

PROACTIVE
Stephen R. Covey

It means more than merely taking initiative. It means that as human beings, we are responsible for our own lives. Our behavior is a function of our decisions, not our conditions. We can subordinate feelings to values. We have the initiative and the responsibility to make things happen.

Look at the word *responsibility*—"response-ability"—the ability to choose your response. Highly proactive people recognize that responsibility. They do not blame circumstances, conditions, or conditioning for their behavior. Their behavior is a product of their own conscious choice, based on values, rather than a product of their conditions, based on feelings.

Because we are, by nature, proactive, if our lives are a function of conditioning or conditions, it is because we have, by conscious decision or by default, chosen to empower those things to control us.

In making such a choice, we become *reactive*. Reactive people are often affected by their physical environment. If the weather is good, they feel good. If it isn't, it affects their attitude and their performance. Proactive people carry their own weather with them.

Whether it rains or shines makes no difference to them. They are value driven; and if their value is to produce good quality work, it isn't a function of whether the weather is conducive to it or not.

Reactive people are also affected by their social environment, by the "social weather." When people treat them well, they feel well; when people don't, they become defensive or protective. Reactive people build their emotional lives around the behavior of others, empowering the weaknesses of other people to control them.

The ability to subordinate an impulse to a value is the essence of the proactive person. Reactive people are driven by feelings, by circumstance, by conditions, by their environment. Proactive people are driven by values—carefully thought about, selected and internalized values.

. . . I admit this is very hard to accept emotionally, especially if we have had years and years of explaining our misery in the name of circumstance or someone else's behavior. But until a person can say deeply and honestly, "I am what I am today because of the choices I made yesterday," that person cannot say, "I choose otherwise."

THINKING SKILLS 47

1. How is our behavior a function of our decisions, not our conditions?

_____

_____

_____

_____

2. Give an example of subordinating feelings to values.

_____

_____

_____

_____

3. How can our lives be a function of conditioning or conditions?

_____

_____

_____

_____

4. How can one be value driven?

_____

_____

_____

_____

5. List three of your most important values.

A. _____

B. _____

C. _____

THINKING SKILLS 48

Can you find the two sides on these cubes that contain exactly the same symbols?

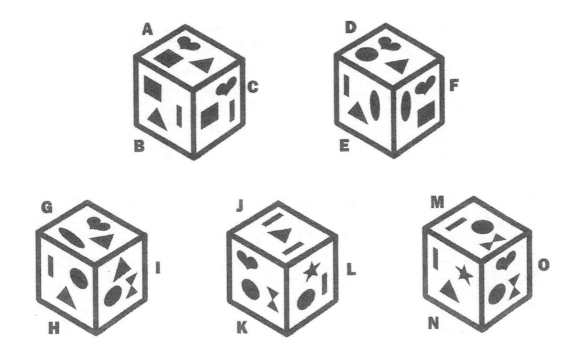

SIDE_____ & SIDE_____are the same.

Mensa Mind Challenge, by Robert Allen, © 1995, 2002 by Carlton Books Limited. Published by Thunder Bay Press, an imprint of the Advantage Publishing Group. Reprinted with permission from Carlton Books, Ltd.

95 PERCENT
Arthur G. Kirn and Marie O'Donahoe Kirn

About 95 percent of us utilize only 5 percent of our potential. Many behavior scientists subscribe to this confronting hypothesis. When we look at the achievements of champions, heroes, and the great, the noble, the self-actualizing, or people under stress or pressure, we are astonished at what they can do. Something in us recognizes our great potential and knows that we can tap it more often than we do.

Surprisingly, many of us are more comfortable and familiar with our weaknesses and limitations than we are with our strengths. Some of us might feel guilty or defensive about not having done more with our abilities than we have. Some of us have a tendency to talk ourselves down and minimize our positive sides.

What can you do? That's a hard question for most of us to answer. It is fairly obvious that you can't plan ahead, think ahead, and make choices for yourself if you are not in touch with yourself and with your real capacities and capabilities.

You have the capability to accomplish many great things in your life. You are a highly intelligent person, even if everyone else in your life has been telling you for years that you are not.

WEEDING YOUR MIND

A man's mind may be likened to a garden, which may be intelligently cultivated or allowed to run wild; but whether cultivated or neglected, it must and will, bring forth. If no useful seeds are put into it, then an abundance of useless weed-seeds will fall therein, and will continue to produce their kind.

Just as a gardener cultivates a plot, keeping it free from weeds, and growing the flowers and fruits which are required, so may a man tend the garden of his mind, weeding out all the wrong, useless, and impure thoughts, and cultivating toward perfection the flowers and fruits of right, useful, and pure thoughts. By pursuing this process, a man sooner or later discovers that he is the master-gardener of his soul, the director of his life. He also reveals, within himself, the laws of thought, and understands, with ever-increasing accuracy, how the thought-forces and mind-elements operate in the shaping of his character, circumstances and destiny.

As A Man Thinketh, James Allen (1864–1912), Dover Publications, Inc.

THINKING SKILLS 49

1. Finish the following: Just as a gardener cultivates a plot, _____

_____

_____

_____

_____

_____

2. What do you think are the main reasons why entry-level employees are fired?

A. _____

B. _____

C. _____

D. _____

E. _____

3. What do you think are five common workplace excuses?

A. _____

B. _____

C. _____

D. _____

E. _____

MAIN REASONS ENTRY-LEVEL EMPLOYEES ARE FIRED

- Missing work = Not being dependable
- Always late = Not being dependable
- Fighting = Not being able to control emotion
- Stealing = Not being dependable or trustworthy
- Negative attitude = Lack of interest
- Being rude and unpleasant to supervisors, coworkers, and customers = Poor customer service skills and poor interpersonal skills.
- Never accepting personal responsibility = Always having an excuse for everything
- Being intoxicated or on drugs = Inability to forego immediate pleasures
- Need constant supervision = Lack of motivation and initiative
- Constant arguing = Inability to get along with others

THE 10 MOST COMMON WORKPLACE EXCUSES

James Bleech

1. It's not my fault.

2. It was someone else's job.

3. Something else came up.

4. I didn't have time.

5. We've never done it that way before.

6. No one told me to do it.

7. I had too many interruptions.

8. If only my supervisor understood.

9. I'll get to it later.

10. No one showed me how to do it.

THINKING SKILLS 50

1. If the sum of the fourth number and the ninth number is greater than the sixth number, write down the sum of the second and seventh number. Otherwise, write down the sum of the first number and tenth number minus the ninth number.

   8   3   9   4   9   7   5   6   2   1

   _____

2. Mrs. Jones has just bought a new washing machine. It takes 20 minutes to wash one T-shirt and one pair of pants. How long will it take her to wash three T-shirts and three pairs of pants?

   _____

3. On which side of a cup is it best to have a handle?

   _____

4. Where do fish keep their money?

   _____

5. I have two coins that add up to 55 cents. One of them is not a nickel. What are the two coins?

   _____

WHEN WE ARE
Dr. Penelope Russianoff

When we are habitually depressed, feeling helpless or worthless, it is as though a terrible weariness overtakes us. And it is easier to stay put than to try and pull ourselves out. Excuses provide the justification for inaction. Excuses are the knife we use to cut the lifelines that people throw us. Excuses are the mask behind which we hide, the crutches on which we lean. We rely on excuses to avoid risk, to explain failure, to resist change, to protect our egos. The excuse is our way of saying: "You see, it's not my fault."

Understanding and solving your emotional bad habits is a difficult task. It is not easy to abandon your cozy excuses. When you dread getting out of bed in the morning, you can invent a dozen reasons why you shouldn't. The disinterest to improve keeps you in a trench of not caring to improve. The emotional force of gravity is all on the side of staying there. Overcoming the disinterest to improve means going directly against what you feel. It means that if you feel worthless, you must use your thinking skills and reasoning skills to develop positive mental attitude. We all have this ability. If you feel rejected, you must get out there and risk rejection again. If you feel helpless, you need to start taking control of your life. All of this is very hard.

If we can clear the first hurdle and rouse ourselves from our disinterest to improve, then we can reverse the emotional gravity. We can make it work for us instead of against us. If we force ourselves to face our problems and do something about them, however depressed we may be, we will probably at some point find ourselves engaged in positive mental and social activities that distract us from absorption in our depression. Sociability displaces gloom. The mind cannot contain both attitudes simultaneously. If we engage in positive social interaction with our family and friends, then for a few hours at least we will not have time to wallow in our negativity.

Commitment. Involvement. Engagement. These are the best medicines against emotional paralysis. Nature made us to be curious, exploring, creative creatures. The disinterest to improve state is an unnatural one. Excuses keep us down. The way to stop making excuses is simply to stop. Set a statue of limitations. Say to yourself: "I wallowed for three months making excuses why I can't improve myself. Time is up. I know it is going to be difficult but I will start immediately." We always have a choice between doing something about our problems and not doing anything about our problems except adding to them.

The road to hell, we are told, is paved with good intentions—and excuses are the paving stones.

EMPLOYMENT NOTES

Situations arise at work and sometimes I do not handle them properly. A good example of this is when another employee will say something to me that I find offensive or hurtful. I take it personally, get angry, and respond in a negative manner. I know better than to respond when I am angry, but it still occurs at times. When I make mistakes, the best way I have found to deal with my mistakes is to remind myself that I failed, that I am not perfect, and that I need to improve.

THINKING SKILLS 51

1. What does success mean to you?

_____

_____

_____

_____

_____

2. Give three reasons why we use excuses.

A._____

_____

B._____

C._____

_____

3. What are three medicines against emotional paralysis?

A._____
B._____
C._____

TO HAVE SUCCEEDED

To laugh often and much;
To win the respect of intelligent people
And the affection of children;
To earn the appreciation of honest critics
And endure the betrayal of false friends;
To appreciate beauty,
To find the best in others;
To leave the world a bit better,
Whether by a healthy child,
A garden patch
Or a redeemed social condition;
To know even one life has breathed easier
Because you have lived.
This is to have succeeded.

Attributed to Ralph Waldo Emerson. Original verse is attributed to Bessie Anderson Stanley.

THE ENEMY

Thomas Wolfe (1900–1938)

I think the enemy is here before us. . . . I think the enemy is *simple selfishness and compulsive greed.* . . . I think the enemy is old as Time, and evil as Hell, and that he has been here with us from the beginning. I think he stole our earth from us, destroyed our wealth, and ravaged and spoiled our land. I think he took our people and enslaved them, that he polluted the fountains of our life, took unto himself the rarest treasures of our own possession, took our bread and left us with a crust, and, not content, for the nature of the enemy is instated—tried finally to take from us the crust.

Of all the foul growths current in the world,
The worst is money. Money drives men from home,
Plunders proud cities, and perverts honest minds
To shameful practice, godlessness and crime.

—Sophocles (496–406 BC)

SUCCESS
Colin Turner

Success is the continuous accomplishment of planned objectives which are worthwhile to the individual.

The majority of people measure their success as compared with others, but genuine success is what people do with their own potential, their development and improvement of it, and must be related to their individual objectives and personal goals.

Success, however, does not lie in the achievement of the goal, although that is what the world would have us consider success, instead it lies in the journey towards the goal.

The great thing is not so much where we are, as Oliver Wendell Holmes said, but in what direction we are moving. Success is a journey; it is the result of attitudes and habits acquired on that journey. It is not so much the product of unusual talents and abilities but learning to put those talents and abilities to use. It is not doing the unusual but doing the commonplace unusually well.

THE 7 LAWS OF SUCCESS
S. A. Swami

1. Keep the objective in sight.

2. Keep studying about your goal.

3. Make adequate preparation.

4. Work with enthusiasm.

5. Be ready for due sacrifice.

6. Do not mind others.

7. Get continuous feedback.

SELF-EXCELLENCE: KEY TO PREVENTIVE STRESS MANAGEMENT & GOAL ORIENTED LIVING, by S. A. Swami, Ph.D., Published by Minibook Publishing Co. Reprinted with permission from Mrs. Swami.

LAWS TO BECOME UNSUCCESSFUL

1. Go through life without trying to accomplish anything.

2. Fear success because you feel you do not deserve it.

3. Never think about what you want to accomplish.

4. Believe that you will never become successful.

5. Lack self-discipline and have no desire to change.

6. Use violence as a problem-solving technique.

7. Feel sorry for yourself and do not accept responsibility for your position in life.

8. Think your life will improve without doing anything to improve it.

9. Live day to day. Give in to your immediate pleasures.

10. Give up on your education.

EMPLOYMENT NOTES

In order to improve your work performance, feedback is very important. Your best source of feedback is from your supervisor. It is acceptable to ask your supervisor how you are performing. This demonstrates that you are dedicated to your job and want to improve. If you get a negative evaluation, do not take it personally, accept it, and do not argue. The next step would be to improve in the negative areas and change the perception of your supervisor about the negative evaluation. You have to be able to take constructive criticism; otherwise, do not ask.

FIVE SHORT CHAPTERS ON CHANGE
Portia Nelson

Chapter 1	I walk down a street. There is a deep hole in the sidewalk. I fall in. I am lost . . . I am helpless. It isn't my fault. It takes forever to find my way out.
Chapter 2	I walk down the same street. There is a deep hole in the sidewalk. I pretend I don't see it. I fall in again. I can't believe I am in this same place. But, it isn't my fault. It still takes a long time to get out.
Chapter 3	I walk down the same street. There is a deep hole in the sidewalk. I see it is there. I still fall in . . . it's a habit . . . but, my eyes are open. I know where I am. It is my fault. I get out immediately.
Chapter 4	I walk down the same street. There is a deep hole in the sidewalk. I walk around it.
Chapter 5	I walk down another street.

This story presents us with a simple truth. We can go on doing the same things over and over again, lamenting our fate or we can look again and decide a new course of action. We can blame the fates for our state of being, or we can be something else. We can view things in the same old way or we can change our point of view.

—Author Unknown, Source Unknown

> *Success is to be measured not so much by the position that one has reached in life as by the obstacles which he has overcome.*
>
> —Booker T. Washington (1856–1915)

DEVELOPING A POSITIVE SELF-IMAGE

- Avoid putting yourself down with negative self-talk.
- Do something nurturing for yourself every day.
- Form mental images of your real self.
- Surround yourself with positive role models.
- Read self-help books that reinforce your emerging positive sense of self.
- Write down ten positive statements about yourself and say them to yourself on a regular basis.

From *7 KINDS OF SMART, REVISED & UPDATED EDITION* by Thomas Armstrong, copyright © 1993, 1999 by Thomas Armstrong. Reprinted with permission from Plume, an imprint of Penguin Group (USA) Inc.

> *When you are classified as "at risk," "disadvantaged," and "underprivileged," they are talking about your income. But don't let this determine your outcome, because your mind is not at risk. Your mind is not disadvantaged, and your mind is not underprivileged.*
>
> —Cleo Fields

THINKING SKILLS 52

1. Write down 10 positive statements about yourself:

A. _____

_____

B. _____

_____

C. _____

_____

D. _____

_____

E. _____

_____

F. _____

_____

G. _____

_____

H. _____

_____

I. _____

_____

J. _____

_____

THINKING SKILLS 53

This one is not as easy as it looks. Can you count how many triangles are in this figure?

Answer: _____

---

10. To become successful on a job, finish what you start. Believe in yourself and don't give up.

- Make it a point to try to never quit a job before you have another job.

- You cannot run from problems you experience on a job.

- The same problems exist on every job.

- Focus on what you want to accomplish.

- You must want to get something out of a job than just a paycheck.

- Just think about how much easier your life would be today if you would have finished everything you ever started.

Many people think that if they were in some other place, or had some other job, they would be happy. Well, that is doubtful. So get as much happiness out of what you are doing as you can and don't put off being happy until some future date.

Remember happiness doesn't depend upon who you are or what you have; it depends solely on what you think.

—Andrew Carnegie (1835–1919)

THINKING SKILLS 54

9 DOTS

Connect all nine dots with four straight lines. You can cross a line, but you cannot retrace a line. Once you begin, you cannot lift your pen or pencil.

● ● ●

● ● ●

● ● ●

PRACTICE DOTS

O O O   O O O   O O O

O O O   O O O   O O O

O O O   O O O   O O O

O O O   O O O   O O O

O O O   O O O   O O O

O O O   O O O   O O O

It is common to look at this puzzle and seek a solution that is inside of an imaginary box placed around the nine dots. The solution to solving the puzzle is outside of the imaginary box.

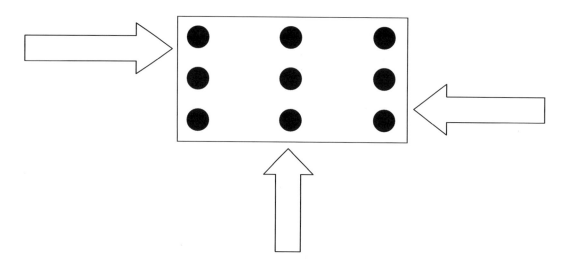

A large percentage of humans never reach their full potential because they live within an imagery box, placing limits on what they can and cannot accomplish. Once you tell yourself that you cannot accomplish something, you will not be able to accomplish it.

The solution to a lot of problems and difficulties you have is also outside of the imaginary box you place on your problem-solving ability. Do not place limits on your problem-solving ability. There are solutions to your problems that you have not yet discovered. Believe in yourself and stay focused on what you want to accomplish and what kind of person you want to become. If you want a bright future with unlimited opportunity, then your education is the foundation you need to build on.

BORN WITH LOVE
Marianne Williamson

Love is what we are born with. Fear is what we learn. The spiritual journey is the unlearning of fear and prejudices and the acceptance of love back in our hearts. Love is the essential reality and our purpose on earth. To be consciously aware of it, to experience love in ourselves and others, is the meaning of life.

Meaning does not lie in things. Meaning lies in us. When we attach value to things that aren't love—the money, the car, the house, the prestige—we are loving things that can't love us back. We are searching for meaning in the meaningless. Money, of itself, means nothing. Material things, of themselves, mean nothing. It's not that they are bad. It's just that they're nothing.

EMPLOYMENT NOTES

Until you can offer a company something in return, don't expect a high per-hour wage. Characteristics that hiring mangers look for are educational level, work experience, work reference from a previous employer, communicational skills, and a friendly demeanor and good attitude. The last three are usually the most important attributes.

PLUG INTO THE POSITIVE CURRENT

Les Brown

We all have the power to choose whether we are going to tap into the negative lower self, or the higher positive self. If sometimes you feel you need to give yourself to resentment, guilt and anger, that is understandable. But if you want to be free of those dark emotions, to rise up and move on, you can do that too.

One of my favorite positively charged people is the jazz singer Jean Carne of Atlanta. Jean co-wrote lyrics for a song she sings called "Infant Eyes." Jean is a nurturing person whom everyone likes to be around. Her song embodies her positively charged approach to life. She dedicated the song to her firstborn child, and in it she says, "Being strong is the one thing in the whole world that will save you." If you tap into that positive strength, you can overcome anything life throws at you, but if you take a negative charge, you let life have its way with you.

I am always amazed at people who react to hardships in their lives by saying, "How can this happen to ME?" Who would they suggest it happen to? Their neighbors? The guy who delivers their mail? Their in-laws?

Many of us act as if we were born with the great expectation that life was going to be easy. Well, if someone told you life was going to be one smooth, easy ride, I've got a special announcement: *THEY LIED!*

Sooner or later in this life, the Messenger of Misery is going to knock on your door. If he isn't at your door right now, he is probably around the corner or just up the street. Be prepared. It is going to happen. And by expecting life to give you a knock now and then, you can handle it as one of life's natural processes. There is no need to panic, to whine or to look for blame. Know that it will come and be prepared to handle it without personalizing it.

THIS, TOO, WILL PASS
Grace Noll Crowell

This, too, will pass. O heart, say it over and over,
Out of your deepest sorrow, out of your grief,
No hurt can last forever, perhaps tomorrow
Will bring relief.

This, too, will pass. It will spend itself, its furry
Will die as the wind dies down with the setting sun;
Assuaged and calm, you will rest again, forgetting
A thing that is done.

Repeat it again and again, oh, heart, for your
comfort;
This, too, will pass, as surely as passed before
The old forgotten pain, and the other sorrows
That once you bore.

As certain as stars at night or dawn after darkness,
Inherent as the lift of the blowing grass,
Whatever your despair or your frustration—
This, too, will pass.

RISK

To laugh is to risk appearing the fool. To weep is to risk being called sentimental. To reach out to another is to risk involvement. To expose feelings is to risk showing your true self. To place your ideas and your dreams before a crowd is to risk being called naive. To love is to risk not being loved in return. To live is to risk dying. To hope is to risk despair, and to try is to risk failure. But risks must be taken, because the greatest risk in life is to risk nothing. The person who risks nothing, does nothing, has nothing, is nothing, and becomes nothing. He may avoid suffering and sorrow, but he simply cannot learn and feel and change and grow and love and live. Chained by things that are certain, he is a slave. He has forfeited his freedom. Only the person who risks is truly free.

A Leo Buscaglia tribute website attributes this quote to Janet Rand who "stepped forward" as the author. It has also been attributed to William Arthur Ward.

QUOTES FOR DISCUSSION

All of the world is full of suffering, it is also full of the overcoming of it.
—Helen Keller (1880–1968)

Character cannot be developed in ease and quiet. Only through experience of trial and suffering can the soul be strengthened, vision cleared, ambition inspired, and success achieved.
—Helen Keller (1880–1968)

A man who stands for nothing will fall for anything.
—Malcolm X (1925–1965)

To you is granted the power of degrading yourself into the lower forms of life, the beasts, and to you is granted the power, contained in your intellect and judgment, to be reborn into the higher forms, the divine.
—Giovanni Pico della Mirandola (1463–1494)

No one ever became extremely wicked suddenly.
—Juvenal, (58 AD–127 AD)

If you damage the character of another person, you damage your own.
—Yoruba proverb

What a man's mind can create, man's character can control.
—Thomas Edison (1847–1931)

The way to overcome the angry man is with gentleness, the evil man with goodness, the miser with generosity and the liar with truth.
—Indian proverb

All that we are is the result of what we have thought. If people speak or act with evil thoughts, pain follows them. If people speak or act with pure thoughts, happiness follows them, like a shadow that never leaves them.
—Siddhartha Gautama (563 BC–483 BC)

To see what is right and not to do it is want of courage.
—Confucius (551 BC–479 BC)

Watch your thoughts, for they become words. Watch your words, for they become actions. Watch your actions, for they become habits. Watch your habits, for they become character. Watch your character, for it becomes your destiny.

—Author Unknown

THINKING SKILLS 55

1. Finish the following statements:
   Meaning does not lie in things. Meaning lies in us.
   When we attach value to things_____

   _____

   _____

   _____

   _____

   _____

   _____

   _____

   _____

2. Remember happiness doesn't depend upon_____

   _____

   _____

   _____

   _____

3. A man who stands for nothing_____

   _____

THINKING SKILLS 56

1. The Yankees and the Indians play five baseball games. They each win three games. There were no ties, forfeits, or disputed games. How is this possible?

_____

2. What animal can jump higher than a house?

_____

3. Imagine you are in a sinking rowboat surrounded by man-eating sharks. How could you survive?

_____

4. You are trapped and the only way out is to choose one of three rooms within the next minute. The first is full of a raging fire, the second is full of assassins with loaded guns, and the third is full of lions that have not eaten in three years. Which room would you choose?

_____

5. What is once in a minute, twice in a moment, and never in a thousand years?

_____

6. What seven-letter word has hundreds of letters in it?

_____

The Velveteen Rabbit
Margery Williams

"What is REAL?" asked the Rabbit one day when they were lying side by side near the nursery fender before Nana came to tidy the room. "Does it mean having things that buzz inside you and a stick-out handle?"

"REAL isn't how you are made," said the Skin Horse. "It's a thing that happens to you. When a child loves you for a long, long time, then you become REAL."

"Does it hurt?" asked the Rabbit.

"Sometimes," said the Skin Horse, for he was always truthful. "When you are REAL you don't mind being hurt."

"Does it happen all at once, like being wound up," he asked, "or bit by bit?"

"It doesn't happen all at once," said the Skin Horse. "It is a process. It takes a long time. That's why it doesn't often happen to people who break easily, or have sharp edges, or have to be carefully kept. Generally, by the time you are REAL, most of your hair has been loved off, and your eyes drop off, and you get loose in the joints and very shabby. But these things don't matter at all because once you are REAL you can't be ugly, except to people who don't understand."

EMPLOYMENT NOTES

Employers do not have time to be babysitters. If you break easily, have sharp edges, or have to be carefully kept, you will not last long on a job. Employers are in business to make money and focus on business-related problems. They will not wait for you to develop your soft skills. They expect all employees to already have developed excellent soft skills.

EMPLOYMENT NOTES

It feels good to be recognized by a supervisor for being a hard worker and an excellent employee. There are many jobs where you will not get this type of recognition. Do not let the lack of recognition affect your productivity. Provide your own recognition, congratulate yourself, use positive self-talk, and keep moving forward.

THINKING SKILLS 57

Rank from 1 to 10 what you want from a job.
If it is not listed, add it at the bottom. (1 = most important)

Interesting work	
Appreciation for your work	
Work that is challenging and meaningful	
Feeling of being part of the company	
Good bosses	
Job security	
Good wages	
Flexibility in hours and dress	
Promotion and growth in the organization	
Good working conditions	
Personal loyalty to employees	
Tactful discipline	
Good benefits package	
A sense that the employer is concerned about you	
Weekends off	
Work days only	

EMPLOYEE SURVEYS

On most employee surveys concerning the top ten things workers value the most, wages are usually in the middle. The top answers are usually:

(a) Appreciation for your work

(b) Feeling of being part of the company

(c) A sense that the employer is concerned about you

SECTION 2

PROBLEM SOLVING AND OTHER COGNITIVE SKILLS

SECTION 2
PROBLEM SOLVING AND OTHER
COGNITIVE SKILLS

The significant problems we face cannot be solved at the same level of thinking we were at when we created them.

—Albert Einstein (1879–1955)

Problems are negative things, unpleasant situations, situations that could improve, things you would rather avoid. A problem exists when an obstacle separates where you are from where you want to be. If you do nothing to solve your problems, they will only cause you more problems in the future. Solving a problem is an opportunity to make your life better.

A teacher once defined problem solving as placing a piece of paper in the corner of the room and trying to jump over it diagonally, from one end to the other end. You want to accomplish something—jumping over the paper—and there is an obstacle in the way, the walls. How can you solve this problem? You could move the walls, which would be very expensive, or you can move the paper away from the corner.

You can view your problems in the same manner, whether they are work-related problems or personal problems. There are solutions to your problems that you have not yet discovered.

It is normal to think that once you get a job, all of your problems will be solved. Getting a job will not solve all of your problems. Getting a job will create a new set of problems. To be successful on a job, you will need to be aware of the possible problems and how to deal with these types of problems. You will need to develop your problem-solving and decision-making skills. On a daily basis, you will be making decisions that will affect your employment. This section will discuss ways in which you can improve these skills.

FACTS ABOUT PERSONAL PROBLEMS

- Everybody has them.
- For a problem to exist, it had to be created.
- If you created a problem, you have the ability to solve it.
- If you are having the same problem over and over, it indicates that you are not willing to change.
- To solve problems, you have to be willing to change.
- Problems are a part of life.
- You will always have problems.
- You will always have the ability to deal with your problems.
- You can decrease your problems by making wise decisions.
- Thinking in terms of consequences will help eliminate many problems.
- Thinking in terms of what you want to accomplish will help guide your consequential decision making.
- Just thinking will solve a lot of problems.
- If you do not know what you want to accomplish, be prepared for a lot of problems.
- If you think that you do not have any problems, you are fooling yourself.
- The only people without problems are in the cemetery.
- Focusing on immediate pleasures is the root of most problems.
- The problem of lacking basic educational skills will grow bigger and faster than almost any other problem you might have.
- A "not-caring attitude" will multiply your problems at an even faster rate.

- To help avoid problems, you have to take responsibility for your actions.
- The problems you have today are the result of the choices you have made in the past.
- Problems you have in the future will be the result of bad choices you make today.
- Every employer has problems; do not add to their problems.
- The more problems you create for your employer, the more problems you are creating for yourself.
- A job will solve more problems than it creates.
- The more problems you have, the more opportunity there is to improve your life.
- You probably do not deserve a lot of problems you are facing, but they are your problems and you are the only one who can find a solution to them.

It is a painful thing to look at your own trouble and know that you yourself, and no one else, has made it.

—Sophocles (496 BC–406 BC)

Misfortunes do not flourish particularly in our path. They grow everywhere.

—Big Elk (1770–1853)

Little minds are tamed and subdued by misfortune; but great minds rise above them.

—Washington Irving (1783–1859)

Acceptance of what has happened is the first step to overcoming the consequences of any misfortune.

—William James (1842–1910)

WHAT MAKES LIFE DIFFICULT
M. Scott Peck, MD

What makes life difficult is that the process of confronting and solving problems is a painful one. Problems, depending upon their nature, evoke in us frustration or grief or sadness or loneliness or guilt or regret or anger or fear or anxiety or anguish or despair. These are uncomfortable feelings, often very uncomfortable, often as painful as any kind of physical pain, sometimes equaling the very worst kind of physical pain. Indeed, it is because of the pain that events or conflicts engender in us all that we call them problems. And since life poses an endless series of problems, life is always difficult and is full of pain as well as joy.

THINKING SKILLS 58

1. What happens twice in a week, once in a year, but never in a day?

_____

2. Star is to rats as reward is to:
   a) mice b) ransom   c) drawer   d) fame

_____

3. Below is a series of numbers. What is the next number in the sequence?

1
11
21
1211
111221
312211
13112221

_____

4. What is three days before the day that is spelled with the most number of letters?

_____

5. From what seven-letter word can you take away two letters and have eight left?

_____

MAJOR CONTRIBUTORS TO PERSONAL PROBLEMS

- Thinking you should always be happy
- Thinking you should have fun every day and night
- Thinking that things will get better by themselves
- Thinking someone is going to save you
- Thinking that a good job will appear out of nowhere
- Making fun of other people
- Looking down on others
- Judging others
- Showing a lack of respect for other human beings
- Not being able to control your emotions
- Thinking money will make you happy
- Not caring about where you will be ten years from now
- Feeling sorry for yourself
- Being angry most of the time
- Not caring
- Blaming your problems on others
- Not believing in yourself
- Negative self-talk
- Thinking your life will not improve
- Being influenced by others
- Abusing drugs and alcohol
- Being dishonest
- Not taking pride in your work
- Giving in to your immediate pleasures

QUOTES FOR DISCUSSION

Be of good cheer. Do not think of today's failures, but of the success that may come tomorrow. You have set yourselves a difficult task, but you will succeed if you persevere; and you will find joy in overcoming obstacles. Remember, no effort that we make to attain something beautiful is ever lost.

—Helen Keller (1880–1968)

A man, as a general rule, owes very little to what he is born with—a man is what he makes of himself.

—Alexander Graham Bell (1847–1922)

Problems are sent to us as gifts.

—Ancient Oriental teaching

The beauty of the soul shines out when a man bears with composure one heavy mischance after another, not because he does not feel them, but because he is a man of high and heroic temper.

—Aristotle (384 BC–322 BC)

When flowing water . . . meets with obstacles on its path, a blockage in its journey, it pauses. It increases in volume and strength, filling up in front of the obstacle and eventually spilling past it. . . .
Do not turn and run, for there is nowhere worthwhile for you to go. Do not attempt to push ahead into the danger . . . emulate the example of the water: Pause and build up your strength until the obstacle no longer represents a blockage.

—I Ching (1000 BC)

It is impossible to live a pleasant life without living wisely and honorably and justly, and it is impossible to live wisely and honorably and justly without living pleasantly. Whenever any one of these is lacking, when, for instance, the man is not able to live wisely, though he lives honorably and justly, it is impossible for him to live a pleasant life.

—Epicurus (341 BC–270 BC)

Life is not a continuum of pleasant choices but of inevitable problems that call for strength, determination, and hard work.

—Indian proverb

When you come to the end of your rope, tie a knot and hang on.

—Franklin D. Roosevelt (1882–1945)

THINKING SKILLS 59

1. Explain the following Albert Einstein quote:
   "The significant problems we face cannot be
   solved at the same level of thinking we were at
   when we created them."

   _____

   _____

   _____

   _____

   _____

   _____

   _____

   _____

2. What does it mean to accept responsibility for
   your problems and your life?

   _____

   _____

   _____

   _____

   _____

   _____

SELF-ESTEEM IS…

Nathaniel Branden, Ph.D.

1. Confidence in our ability to think and to cope with the basic challenges of life

2. Confidence in our right to be happy, the feeling of being worthy, deserving, entitled to assert our needs and wants and to enjoy the fruits of our efforts

OUR CHOICES AFFECT OUR SELF-ESTEEM
Nathaniel Braden, Ph.D.

The choices we make concerning the operation of our consciousness have enormous effects for our lives in general and our self-esteem in particular. Consider the impact on our lives and on our sense of self entailed by the following options:

Thinking   versus Non-thinking

Focusing   versus Non-focusing

Awareness versus Unawareness

Clarity   versus Obscurity or Vagueness

Respect for reality versus Avoidance of reality

Respect for facts versus Indifference to facts

Respect for truth versus Rejection of truth

Perseverance in the effort to understand
       versus Abandonment of the effort

Loyalty in action to our professed convictions
      versus Disloyalty—the issue of integrity

Honesty with self versus Dishonesty

Self-confrontation versus Self-avoidance

Openness to new knowledge versus   Closed-mindedness

Willingness to see and correct errors
                              versus   Determination to error

Concern with being agreeable
                          versus   Disregard of contradictions

Reason   versus   Irrationalism; respect for logic, consistency, coherence, and evidence versus disregard or defiance of evidence

Loyalty to the responsibility of consciousness
                          versus   Betrayal of that responsibility

If one wishes to understand the foundations of genuine self-esteem, this list is a good place to begin.

No one could seriously suggest that our sense of our competence to cope with the challenge of life or our sense of our goodness could remain unaffected, over time, by the pattern of our choices in regard to the above options.

EMPLOYMENT NOTES

If you are staying focused and you make a mistake at work, don't worry about it. Learn from your mistake and move on. Worry if you keep making the same mistake over and over.

YOUR POWER OF CHOICE
Colin Turner

Your power of choice, your ultimate freedom must be your greatest power. You have the power to think whatever you choose to allow into your head. The freedom of choice is your birthright; your circumstances have nothing to do with your destiny, they are merely the result of past choices or non-choice.

Your thoughts are your own, uniquely yours to keep, change, share or contemplate. No one else can get inside your head and experience your own thoughts. You do, indeed, control your thoughts, and your brain is your own to use as you wish. You cannot have a feeling or emotion without first having experienced a thought. Take away your brain and your ability to "feel" has gone as a feeling is a physical reaction to a thought.

If you can control your thoughts you can determine your feelings and you can choose how you respond or act in a particular situation. This means that you can no longer blame circumstances for any situation you find yourself in. If we can begin to examine our lives in the light of choices we have made or, more significantly, failed to make then we can start to see that we are the person responsible for how we feel. Accept that you are the sum total of your choices made to date and, therefore, with new choices you can decide to be, have or do anything you want for the future.

Life does not require us to be consistent, cruel, patient, helpful, angry, rational, thoughtless, loving, rash, open-minded, neurotic, careful, rigid, tolerant, wasteful, rich, downtrodden, gentle, sick, considerate, funny, ignorant, healthy, greedy, beautiful, lazy, responsive, foolish, sharing, pressured, intimate, hedonistic, industrious, manipulative, insightful, capricious, wise, selfish, kind or sacrificed. Life does, however, require us to live with the consequences of our choices.

THE POWER TO CHANGE
Les Brown

I will never forget the day the principal came into my fifth-grade classroom while we were clowning around, throwing paper, running, turning chairs over, acting wild. The teacher had left the room unattended and the class went crazy, until the principal showed up.

She was outraged. Trouble had been brewing for several of us for some time. And it was at this moment that the principal made a decision that was to have a powerful impact on my life. In her anger, she began pointing at the most troublesome students and calling us names. "These students are stupid, dumb, retarded. They don't need to be here," she said. "They need to be put back."

"I want that one, that one and that one." She pointed at about six students, including me. I remember the look on her face, the anger and the disgust her expression held. She was set on teaching us a lesson; on punishing us and making us pay. I remember the fear and hurt welling up inside of me.

I said, "No, you are making a mistake! I'm not stupid!"

With that, they took us out of the fifth-grade class and put us back in the fourth grade as special education students. I was kept in that category all through high school. It has taken me a long time to escape that label.

In adulthood, much of my drive to succeed has been fueled by the devastating memory of that day in class when I was judged to be "slow" and without much promise. That memory still pricks at me, a memory that for a time shamed and stunted me but now drives me always to reaffirm my sense of who I am.

Later, the principal told my mother that they had put me back a grade for my own good. She said they were trying to help me. She was very courteous and persuasive. My mother, who had little formal schooling, went along. She felt she had no choice.

THINKING SKILLS 60

1. UNUSUAL TRAIT

What unusual trait does each of the following words have in common?

Telephone
Shorten
Canine
Height
Feminine
Overweight
Often
Throne

2. A PARTICULARLY PERPLEXING PARAGRAPH

This is an unusual paragraph. It has a trait not found in many paragraphs of this
many words. Can you find out what it is? It's not as hard as you might think.
Just look and study. I know you can do it. Good luck!

3. ALL IN THE FAMILY

Tommy's mother has three children represented by the coins below. The first
child is named Penny. The second is named Nicole. What is the name of the
third child (male name)?

ANSWER:_____

Reprinted, with permission from the book *Are You Smart, or What?* by Pat Battaglia

6 STEPS TO PROBLEM SOLVING

1. Define the problem.

2. Get the facts. Focus on the important facts.

3. Think of different solutions to the problem.

4. Analyze the solutions and come up with a plan.

5. Carry out your plan.

6. Evaluate the effects of your plan.

FIRST PROBLEM-SOLVING STEP

1. DEFINE THE PROBLEM.

- What is the problem?
- Be clear with yourself when identifying the problem.
- Make sure that the problem you are focusing on is not a symptom of a larger problem you are overlooking.
- Decide what you want to achieve and how this discomfort is holding you back.

The way we see the problem is the problem.
—Stephen Covey

NEW ELEVATORS
J. Baer and J. C. Kaufman

The owner of an office building in a major city had a problem. His building had only two elevators and his tenants complained these elevators were much too slow. Some were even threatening to move out. The owner asked an elevator company what it would cost to speed up the elevators. They came up with possible solutions:

- Retrofitting the two old elevators to make them faster
  COST: 1 million dollars

- Build two brand new elevators
  COST: 4 million dollars

241

The owner did not want to spend so much money but he could not afford to lose his tenants. He was talking his problem over with a friend one day and he wondered if there might be some other way to speed up the elevators.

His friend suggested that he think about his problem differently. "You're trying to solve the problem of how to make the elevator faster. But the real problem is how to keep your tenants happy and especially how to keep them from being upset by the elevators. Making the elevators go faster might solve the problem of how to keep your tenants from being upset, but I think there might be an easier way. "Why not just install large mirrors on all the landings where people wait for elevators? Then it won't seem like such a long wait, and your tenants won't mind the time they spend waiting for the elevator."

It worked—in fact, it worked so well that it's hard these days to find an elevator where the landings aren't decked in full-length mirrors. We are such a vain species. . . .

The way we think about a problem can have a major impact on the kinds of solutions we conceive

Baer, J. & Kaufman, J.C. (in press). *BEING CREATIVE INSIDE AND OUTSIDE THE CLASSROOM.* Rotterdam: Sense Publishers. Reprinted with permission from John Baer.

CREATIVE THINKERS
J. Baer and J. C. Kaufman

Creative thinkers see opportunities where others see only problems.

* You recognize a situation that could be improved.
* You don't know how to improve the problem

WHAT IS THE FIRST STEP: You must be willing to devote some time to trying to find ways to make the situation better.
1. STATE THE PROBLEM
   - Do not limit yourself by the way you define the problem
   - Make sure the problem you are working on is truly the problem you want to solve

STORY ABOUT OFFICE BUILDING.
Trying to solve the problem of how to make the elevator service faster. The real problem was how to keep the tenants happy and how to keep them from being upset by the elevators.

We tend to find solutions that fit problems as we have defined them. The way we think about problems can have a major impact on the kinds of solutions we conceive.

EXAMPLE

I have mice in my house. I have set traps, but I still have mice.

I might think of the problem *"HOW MIGHT I BUILD A BETTER MOUSE TRAP"*

I would be limiting my range of possible solutions by defining the problem in such a small frame.

I need to widen the problem definition.

HOW MIGHT I BE MORE EFFECTIVE IN CATCHING MICE?

Possible solution includes better mouse traps, but also such things as cats, poisons, and devices other than traps.

I continue to widen the problem definition.

HOW MIGHT I AVOID HAVING MICE IN MY HOUSE?

Possible solution now includes all of the above, plus finding and filling the holes, or moving to another house. It also includes solutions such as cleaning up areas outside of you house that could be a nesting area for mice.

Widen again.

HOW MIGHT I NOT BE BOTHERED BY MICE?

Again the solution would include all of the above plus would allow possibilities as ways to get along with mice or finding ways not to notice them.

GOALS:
1. Do not limit yourself by the way you define the problem.
2. Make sure that the problem you are working on is truly the problem you want to solve.

Magic words to begin every problem.

1. "IN WHAT WAYS MIGHT I...?"

2. "HOW MIGHT I...?"

When you ask yourself these questions, it directs your problem solving energies towards solutions rather than towards complaints or restatements of what bothers you about the situation. It will push you towards solutions that focus on what you really want. It helps to avoid focusing on what's wrong with a situation rather than on how you might make it better.

Baer, J. and Kaufman, J.C. (in press). *BEING CREATIVE INSIDE AND OUTSIDE THE CLASSROOM.* Rotterdam: Sense Publishers. Reprinted with permission from John Baer.

THINKING SKILLS 61

1. List six ways in which you can avoid stepping on ants.

A. _____

B. _____

C. _____

D. _____

E. _____

F. _____

2. List six ways in which you can use dust.

A. _____

B. _____

C. _____

D. _____

E. _____

F. _____

THINKING SKILLS 62

1. Explain and give an example of the following quote: "Creative thinkers see opportunities where others see only problems."

_____

_____

_____

_____

_____

_____

2. What are the magic words to begin every problem?

A. _____

B. _____

3. Why are these words important to use?

_____

_____

_____

_____

_____

MAKE SURE THAT THE PROBLEM YOU ARE FOCUSING ON IS NOT A SYMPTOM OF A LARGER PROBLEM YOU ARE OVERLOOKING.

PROBLEM	LARGER PROBLEM BEING OVERLOOKED
Can't find a job	Dishonest: Caught stealing on last job
Not getting promoted	Does not get along with other employees
Not liked by boss	Not dependable
Always tired	Not focused: Staying out late every night
Underpaid	Does not take pride in work
Not liked by other employees	Lazy
Always late	Does not plan properly
Always getting fired	Bad attitude
Not being given any authority	Lack of an education
Never get to work overtime	Not a team player
Never assigned easy jobs	Disrespectful, loud, and disruptive
Always being assigned jobs away from customers	Poor communication skills

SECOND PROBLEM-SOLVING STEP

2. GET THE FACTS. FOCUS ON THE IMPORTANT FACTS.

- Look at all the facts and important criteria that are involved with the problem. (This would involve everything you have observed about the problem and how the problem has affected you.)
- Be honest with yourself.
- Seek other perspectives.
- Do not make assumptions about the problem or solution.
- Be positive. View your problem as an opportunity to make things better and not as an obstacle.

OBSTACLES AND OPPORTUNITIES

Speaker's Idea File, Ragan Communications, Inc.

Many years ago, a large American shoe manufacturer sent two sales representatives out to different parts of the Australian outback to see if they could drum up some business among the aborigines. Sometime later, the company received telegrams from both agents.

The first sales representative viewed the situation as an *obstacle*, and wrote, "No business here. Natives don't wear shoes."

The second sales representative viewed the situation as an *opportunity*, and wrote, "Great opportunity here. Natives don't wear shoes."

THINKING SKILLS 63

OBSERVATIONS, ASSUMPTIONS, AND INFERENCES WORKSHEET

A businessman had just turned off the lights in the store when a man appeared and demanded money. The owner opened a cash register. The contents of the cash register were scooped up, and the man sped away. A member of the police force was notified promptly.

Based on the story above, are the following statements true, false, or not enough information?
(T) TRUE = STATEMENT IS TRUE
(F) FALSE = STATEMENT IS FALSE
(?) = NOT ENOUGH INFORMATION IS PROVIDED IN THE STORY TO BE CERTAIN WHETHER THE STATEMENT IS TRUE OR FALSE

T F ? 1. A man appeared after the owner had turned off his store lights.

T F ? 2. The robber was a man.

T F ? 3. The man did not demand money.

T F ? 4. The man who opened the cash register was the owner.

T F ? 5. The store owner scooped up the contents of the cash register and ran away.

T F ? 6. Someone opened a cash register.

T F ? 7. After the man who demanded the money scooped up the contents of the cash register, he
ran away.

T F ? 8. While the cash register contained money, the story does not state how much.

T F ? 9. The robber demanded money of the owner.

T F ? 10. The story concerns a series of events in which only three persons are referred to: the
owner of the store, a man who demanded money, and a member of the police force.

Before us lie two paths—honesty or dishonesty. The ignorant embark on the dishonest path; the wise on the honest. For when you help others, you help yourself; when you hurt others, you hurt yourself. Those who remain honest know the truth: character overshadows money, trust rises above fame. And honesty is still the best policy.

—Chilon of Sparta (sixth century BC)

QUOTES FOR DISCUSSION

Honesty is the first chapter in the book of wisdom.
—Thomas Jefferson (1743–1826)

Honesty is the beginning of education.
—John Ruskin (1819–1900)

The true measure of life is not length, but honesty.
—John Lyly (1554–1606)

If you tell the truth, you don't have to remember anything.
—*Mark Twain (1835–1910)*

Honesty is the best policy. If I lose my honor, I lose myself.
—William Shakespeare (1564–1616)

I hope I shall possess firmness and virtue enough to maintain what I consider the most enviable of all titles, the character of an honest man.
—George Washington (1732–1799)

It is impossible to live a pleasant life without living wisely and honorably and justly, and it is impossible to live wisely and honorably and justly without living pleasantly. Whenever any one of these is lacking, when, for instance, the man is not able to live wisely, though he lives honorably and justly, it is impossible for him to live a pleasant life.
—Epicurus (341 BC–270 BC)

Dishonest people conceal their faults from themselves as well as others, honest people know and confess them.
—Christian Nevell Bovee (1820–1904)

"Why is everyone here so happy except me?"

"Because they have learned to see goodness and beauty everywhere," said the Master.

"Why don't I see goodness and beauty everywhere?"

"Because you cannot see outside of you what you fail to see inside."

THIRD PROBLEM-SOLVING STEP

3. THINK OF DIFFERENT SOLUTIONS TO THE PROBLEM.

- View the problem and its solutions in as many different ways as possible.
- Collect as many ideas as you can about different solutions.
- Do not prejudge any possible solutions.

THINKING SKILLS 64

1. TIE A KNOT

Take hold of each end of a string. Once you have hold of the string, you can't let go. You cannot pass it from one finger to another.

Now, tie a knot in the string.

2. PICK THE NUMBER

From the following numbers, pick the one that has the least in common with the others:

1) THIRTEEN
2) ONE
3) THIRTY-ONE

There is a story about two hikers who encounter a tiger.

The first man said, "There is no point in running because the tiger is faster than either of us."

The second man replied, "It is not about whether the tiger is faster than either of us. It is about whether I'm faster than you. And with that, he ran away."

—Author Unknown, Source Unknown

EMPLOYMENT NOTES

This is a funny and creative solution to the problem the two hikers encountered. The drawback to the solution is that it is opportunistic and self-serving. He was only thinking about himself without any reference to moral principle. You will advance much further in the workplace by not using this type of problem-solving technique. Always be considerate of your fellow employees.

PERCEPTION AFFECTS OUR THOUGHT PROCESS

Perception

Perception is defined as the process through which people receive, organize, and interpret information from their environment. The accuracy of a person's perception influences responses to a specific situation. Major factors influencing the perceptual process are the person's values, past experiences, personality, attitudes, and needs. Our decision-making process is guided by our perception. If our perception of a person, surrounding environment, or situation is distorted, our decision making will be distorted. Two people can look at the same situation and view it differently. This realization can help you in your decision-making process. An example of distorted perception is a person who has no priorities in life and sustains the chronic belief that something better will come along without putting out any effort and without having to sacrifice any immediate pleasures.

Our emotions can interfere with our perception. People who think with their emotions and do not think with their minds will always have difficulties making wise decisions.

Wise decision making is based on your priorities and goals, and the consequences of your decision. Priorities are the things that are most important in your life. Your goals will be directly related to your priorities. You satisfy your priorities by achieving your goals. You will use your priorities and goals as a guide in making wise decisions. You have to form your own goals and priorities.

Be prepared to sacrifice in order to get what you want out of life. You cannot have it both ways. If you expect to have a good time every night while you are young and neglect your education, you pay for it three times over when you get older. You will have trouble finding and keeping a job, you will have trouble supporting your family, you will have trouble with adequate health care, you will have transportation problems, and the list goes on. So take the time that is necessary now to secure your future. It has been estimated that for every year wasted after you are seventeen years old, it takes 2.5 years to catch up. This means that if you waste five years, it would take 12.5 years to catch up. A lot of students are wasting time before they are seventeen years old, which increases the catch-up time. Make wise decisions now and secure a good future.

Every day of your life, you will be making decisions. The position you are in today is a result of the decisions you have made in the past. The decisions you make today and tomorrow will determine your future. Poor decisions will limit your job choices. A police record, drug abuse, or dropping out of school will prevent you from being hired by many companies. Your career path will become very narrow and limited to just a few industries with lower-paying jobs. Many companies do background checks, reference checks, and drug testing before hiring employees. Do not limit the choices you will have in the future by making unwise choices today. The better decisions you make today, the more options you will have in the future. All of your decisions do have consequences.

EMPLOYMENT NOTES

Employees always misuse the terms "suck-up" and "favorite." A "suck-up" or "favorite" is not an employee who is dedicated, hardworking, and friendly with the supervisors and managers. It is admirable to be friendly with the people who control your pay and job. A "suck-up" or "favorite" is a person who is opportunistic and self-serving; they are friendly to supervisors and management with the intent of doing less work than the other employees and getting easier job assignments and better schedules. A "suck-up" or "favorite" is not dedicated and hardworking. Please do not get these terms confused.

THINKING SKILLS 65

1. With what vegetable do you throw away the outside, cook the inside, eat the outside, and throw away the inside?

_____

2. The clerk in a butcher shop is six-foot-one. What does he weigh?

_____

3. A man and a dog traveled down a street. The man rode, yet walked. What was the dog's name?

_____

4. How can you make seven even?

_____

5. Divide 30 by 1/2 and add 10. What is the answer?

_____

THINKING SKILLS 66

Answer each question from your own point of view.

1. Jim has a very good-paying job. How much is Jim paid per year?_____

2. Janus is middle-aged. How old is Janus?_____

3. Ernestine dropped out of school very early. In what grade did she drop out?_____

4. Thomas had a high utility bill last month. How much was his utility bill last month?_____

5. Cecile got a job paying a high per-hour rate. How much is Cecile paid per hour?_____

6. Leroy has work for the same company for a long time. How long has Leroy worked for the same company?

   _____

7. Derrick was late for work. How many minutes late was Derrick?_____

8. Benny has an excellent grade point average. What is his grade point average?_____

EMPLOYMENT NOTES

You might perceive yourself to be an excellent employee. Your boss might view your performance differently. Two people can view the same situation differently. You have to take an inventory of your performance in order to evaluate whether your perception might be distorted. The best way to do this is to ask your boss for his or her opinion about your performance and ask how you can improve your performance. Even if you do not agree, it is the perception of the boss that matters.

EMPLOYMENT NOTES

Your coworkers and supervisors will have good and bad days on a job. If someone responds to you in a negative manner, do not take it personally and do not let it affect your mood and attitude. Do not be like all the other employees. Be better than all the other employees.

FOURTH PROBLEM-SOLVING STEP

4. ANALYZE THE SOLUTIONS AND COME UP WITH A PLAN.

- Note the good and bad points of each solution.
- Eliminate negative side effects as much as possible.
- Investigate the different factors involved with each solution.
- Write down the advantages, disadvantages, and how each solution will affect your desired outcome.
- Are there more advantages or disadvantages?
- After analyzing all your possible solutions, select the one you feel is most likely to solve the problem in the long-term.
- Does the solution seem workable in relation to the problem?
- This will be your plan to best meet your desired outcome.

THINKING SKILLS 67

A professional carpet-layer stepped back to admire his customary flawless work. While surveying the installed carpet, he reached into his shirt pocket for a cigarette and realized they were missing. At the same time, he noticed a lump under the carpet, about the size of a cigarette package. Frustrated with his carelessness, the carpet layer realized he was in a predicament. There was no way to retrieve his cigarette package from under the attached carpet without tearing-up and replacing the entire carpet.

What would you do about the small lump in the carpet?

_____

_____

_____

THINKING SKILLS 68

Each question consists of five drawings lettered A, B, C, D, and E. Four of the drawings are exactly alike; one is slightly different. Select the one drawing that is different.

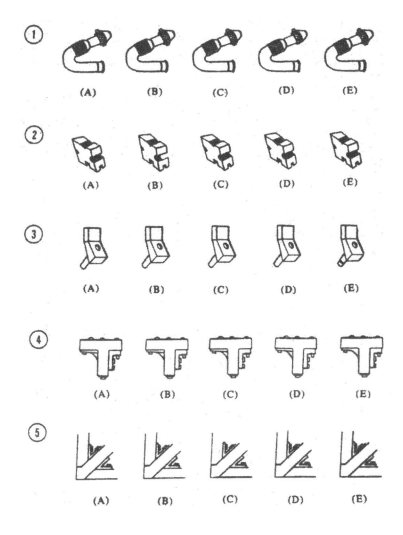

DECISION MAKING

Decision making is part of the problem-solving process. Decision making is simply choosing from among alternatives. You make hundreds of decisions each day: what time to wake up, what to wear, what and where to eat, what to do, what music to listen to, whom to be with, where to work, and so on. Your decisions shape your life. You begin to grow and develop as an adult once you can accept the truth that you are what you are today because of the choices you have made in the past and the choices you make today will shape your future.

To make wise decisions, your decision-making process should be based on your values and priorities, on what is important to you, on what you want to accomplish, and on the consequences of the decision. Control your own decisions and do not let your emotions control your decisions.

Your ability to make wise decisions will never improve unless you formulate your own values. The most important value you can develop is honesty. The first person you have to be honest with is yourself. Do you believe that you can accomplish more than what you have? How often do you lie to other people? Do you ever steal? Do you have to lie in order to get out of trouble? If you are an honest person, you do not cheat, steal, or lie. In order to be an honest person, do not put yourself in a situation in which you have to lie. It is very hard to be an honest person. Honesty is something no one can ever take from you.

When making a decision, always be aware of what is important to you in life and what you want to accomplish in life. Both of these factors should influence your decision. Finally, and just as important, assess the consequences of your decision. All decisions have consequences. Keep your assessment of the consequences in line with what you are trying to accomplish.

IT IS OUR OWN MENTAL ATTITUDE
Swami Vivekananda (1863–1902)

It is our own mental attitude which makes the world what it is for us. Our thoughts make things beautiful, our thoughts make things ugly. The whole world is in our own minds. Learn to see things in the proper light. First, believe in this world—that there is meaning behind everything. Everything in the world is good, is holy and beautiful. If you see something evil, think that you are not understanding it in the right light. Throw the burden on yourself!

QUOTES FOR DISCUSSION

The value of life is not in the length of days, but in the use we make of them; a man may live long yet very little.

—Michel de Montaigne (1533–1592)

There is no value in life except what you choose to place upon it and no happiness in any place except what you bring to it yourself.

—Henry David Thoreau (1817–1862)

Of all the properties which belong to honorable men, not one is so highly prized as that of character.

—Henry Clay (1777–1852)

The real voyage of discovery consists not in seeking new landscapes, but in having new eyes.

—Marcel Proust (1871–1922)

Things are not always as they seem; the first appearance deceives many.
—Phaedrus (15 BC–50 AD)

All of our knowledge has its origin in our perception.
—Leonardo da Vinci (1452–1519)

With your spirit open and unconstructed, look at things from a higher point of view.

—Miyamoto Mustache (1584–1645)

Is it so bad then to be misunderstood? Pythagoras was misunderstood, and Socrates, and Jesus, and Luther, and Copernicus, and Galileo, and Newton, and every pure and wise spirit that ever took flesh. To be great is to be misunderstood.

—Ralph Waldo Emerson (1803–1882)

Always continue the climb. It is possible for you to do whatever you choose, if you first get to know who you are and are willing to work with a power that is greater than ourselves to do it.

—Ella Wheeler Wilcox (1850–1919)

We cannot work for others without working for ourselves.
Doing your work just a little better than anyone else gives you the margin of success.

—Jean-Jacques Rousseau (1712–1778)

THINKING SKILLS 69

1. A farmer had 17 sheep. All but 9 died. How many did he have left?

   _____

2. What is the frequently used English word containing "OOKKEE" in the exact order?

   _____

3. Name ten things you can wear on your feet that begin with the letter "S."

   _____

   _____

   _____

   _____

4. What do you sit on, sleep on, and brush your teeth with?

   _____

5. I am going to place a piece of regular-sized paper on the floor and I will stand on one side and have a volunteer stand on the other side. Once we stand on each side of the paper, the volunteer will not be able to touch me.
   How is this possible?

   _____

WE CAN MAKE RATIONAL OR IRRATIONAL CHOICES
Nathaniel Branden, Ph.D.

We are the one species who can formulate a vision of what values are worth pursuing—and then pursue the opposite. We can decide that a given course of action is rational, morale, and wise—and then suspend consciousness and proceed to do something else. We are able to monitor our behavior and ask if it is consistent with our knowledge, convictions, and ideals—and we are also able to evade asking that question. The option of thinking or not thinking.

If I have reason to know that alcohol is dangerous to me and I nonetheless take a drink, I must first turn down the light of consciousness. If I know that cocaine has cost me my last three jobs and I nonetheless choose to take a snort, I must first blank out my knowledge, must refuse to see what I see and know what I know. I recognize that I am in a relationship that is destructive to my dignity, ruinous for my self-esteem, and dangerous to my physical well-being. If I nonetheless choose to remain in it, I must drown out awareness, fog my brain, and make myself functionally stupid. Self-destruction is an act best performed in the dark.

FIFTH PROBLEM-SOLVING STEP

5. CARRY OUT YOUR PLAN.

- Do not mind your skeptics.
- Believe in your plan.
- Focus on your plan.
  Even if you are on the right track, you will get run over if you just sit there.

  —Will Rogers (1879–1935)

Nothing is more difficult, and therefore more precious, than to be able to decide.

Create a definite plan for carrying out your desire and begin at once, whether you ready or not, to put this plan into action.

Action is the real measure of intelligence.

Don't wait. The time will never be just right.

—Napoleon (1769–1821)

THINKING SKILLS 70

There are 52 frogs sitting on a log in a lake. Nine of the frogs make the bold decision to jump in. How many frogs are left on the log?

THINKING

Walter D. Wintle

If you think you are beaten, you are.
If you think you dare not, you don't.
If you like to win but think you can't
It is almost certain you won't.

If you think you'll lose, you're lost.
For out of the world we find
Success begins with a fellows' will.
It's all in the state of mind.

If you think you are outclassed, you are.
You've got to think high to rise;
You've got to be sure of yourself before
You can ever win a prize.

Life's battles don't always go
To the stronger or faster man;
But sooner or later the man who wins
Is the man who thinks he can.

THINKING SKILLS 71

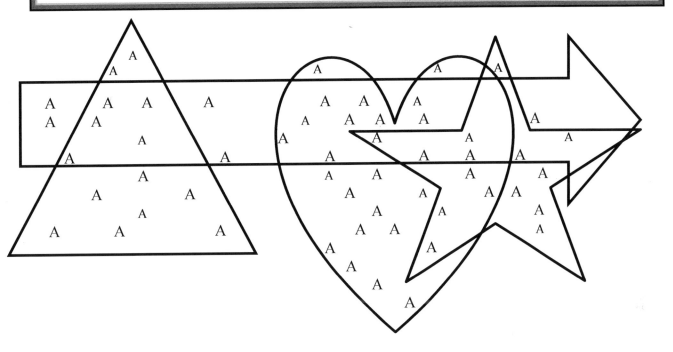

How many A's are:

_____1. In the triangle, but not in the arrow?

_____2. In the star, but not in the heart or arrow?

_____3. In the heart, but not in the arrow or star?

_____4. In the arrow, but not in the heart or star?

_____5. Common to the star and heart, but not to the arrow?

_____6. Common to the arrow and star, but not to the heart?

_____7. Common to the heart and arrow, but not to the star?

_____8. In the star and the heart, but not in both?

_____9. In the arrow and the star, but not in both?

_____10. In the triangle and heart, but not in the arrow or star?

SKEPTICS ARE NEVER SATISFIED

When Mr. Fulton first showed off his new invention, the steamboat, skeptics were crowded on the bank, yelling, "It'll never start, it'll never start!"

It did. It got going with a lot of clanking and groaning, and as it made its way down the river, the skeptics were quiet.

For one minute.

Then they started shouting, "It'll never stop, it'll never stop!"

From a commencement speech delivered by Scott Jacobson
Source: Speaker's Idea File, Ragan Communications, Inc.

EMPLOYMENT NOTES

There are going to be times at work when you get your feelings hurt. It could be from being overlooked for a promotion, not getting a large enough pay raise, or somebody says something offensive to you. If you react with a bad attitude, or become angry, or complain, you are letting whatever happened control you. As William Ward often said, "The pessimist complains about the wind; the optimist expects it to change; the realist adjusts the sails." Adjust your sail and cope with it. Remind yourself that nothing bad lasts forever. Things will change. Be patient and perform your job with a positive attitude.

EMPLOYMENT NOTES

When you start a new job, a lot of your coworkers will have already developed a working relationship with one another. Don't expect to be accepted immediately by your fellow employees. Don't get your feelings hurt by not being accepted right away. Prove yourself and the acceptance will follow.

STUMBLING BLOCKS TO SUCCESS

S. A. Swami, Ph.D.

1. Fear of failure

2. Failure attitude

3. Lack of motivation

4. Ill-defined goals

5. Lack of faith in your plan

6. Lack of incentive

7. Lack of self-discipline

SELF-EXCELLENCE: KEY TO PREVENTIVE STRESS MANAGEMENT & GOAL ORIENTED LIVING, by S. A. Swami, Ph.D., Published by Minibook Publishing Co. Reprinted with permission from Mrs. Swami

SIXTH PROBLEM-SOLVING STEP

6. EVALUATE THE EFFECTS OF YOUR PLAN.

- Verify whether the problem has been resolved and what progress has been made toward resolving the problem.
- You might have to revise your plan if you are not getting your desired outcomes.
- If you are not satisfied with the results, start over.
- There is nothing wrong with making a mistake in the problem-solving model.
- Keep striving to reach your goals.
- The biggest mistake you can make is giving up.

To improve is to change; to be perfect is to change often.

—Winston Churchill (1874–1965)

One thing is sure. We have to do something. We have to do the best we know how at the moment...If it doesn't turn out right, we can modify it as we go along.

—Franklin D. Roosevelt (1882–1945)

Whatever course you decide upon, there is always someone to tell you that you are wrong. There are always difficulties arising which tempt you to believe that your critics are right. To map out a course of action and follow it to an end requires courage.

—Ralph Waldo Emerson, (1803–1882)

A group of people stand at a riverbank and suddenly hear the cries of a baby. Shocked, they see an infant floating—drowning—in the water. One person immediately dives in to rescue the child. But as this is going on, yet another baby comes floating down the river, and then another! People continue to jump in to save the babies and then see that one person has started to walk away from the group still on shore. Accusingly, they shout, "Where are you going?" The response: "I'm going upstream to stop whoever's throwing babies into the river."

—Author Unknown, Source Unknown

LETTERS FROM PRISON

D.K.W.
Serving 85 years

Beliefs are the fundamental tools we employ to guide our actions. Our belief systems are formed from our direct as well as our indirect experiences. By questioning and evaluating our experiences, we are better able to grasp a situation, control it, overcome obstacles and hardships, and discard or modify previously held beliefs into more accurate ones. Our problem solving skills are enhanced when we act in accordance with our beliefs. The more accurate our beliefs, the better able we are to predict, prepare for, and alleviate future problems.

I have learned, even under the gravest conditions, I always have the freedom of choice. My previous belief that the wild action of others precluded my behaving morally and responsibly was a convenient albeit illusory way of distancing myself from personal accountability. I have learned to view life as it actually is and not as I wish it to be. I am now my own harshest critic and strictest disciplinarian. In changing my thinking process, I have lost any number of acquaintanceships but have gained friendships, confidence, self-esteem, ambition, knowledge, understanding, and absolutes. I have also gained this self-evident truth: A higher level of genuine learning begets a higher level of humanity.

BORN TO SUCCEED
Colin Turner

Whatever you believe with feeling becomes your reality. You have the power within you to make your world your reality, just what you want it to be. Every human being wants success, yet the majority of every generation does not give themselves a chance because they believe that whatever they undertake, it will not turn out how they want it to. Disbelief certainly goes hand in hand with failure to achieve.

So many people don't even know what they want and they believe that they have to accept their lives as they are. Those who do have an inclination of what they want, believe they won't achieve it or believe they don't deserve it. It has been said many times that whatever the human mind can conceive and believe can be achieved. The key ingredient for success is believing and true success starts with believing in yourself.

THINKING SKILLS 72

1. SUPPOSE a total stranger approached you with this proposition:

"I want to offer you something that can guarantee you success. It is lightweight, portable, requires no electricity or batteries, it will gather all the facts you want on any given subject, it will weigh the evidence and arrive at a sound decision. Properly maintained, it will investigate anything you wish, it will keep a permanent file of every bit of information it collects, total up figures, provide profitable insights, and render precise judgments. It will build up your vocabulary, teach you anything you want to know, and warn you of impending dangers. With it, you can win the admiration of your peers, predict the future with an astonishing degree of accuracy, and avoid many of the pitfalls of life. It will enable you to sit at the feet of wise men long dead, communicate with those you cannot see, and learn from the mistakes of others. It weighs three pounds and it's free!"

—Author Unknown, Source Unknown

What do you think it is?_____

2. If *folk* is spelled F-O-L-K and *joke* is spelled J-O-K-E, how do you spell the word for the white of an egg?

3. You have two pencils—a good one and a cheap one. The good one cost $1.00 more than the cheap one. You spend $1.10 for both. How much did the cheap one cost?

THINKING SKILLS 73

1. What are three consequences of not being a dependable worker?

A. _____

B. _____

C. _____

2. What are three consequences of being a dependable worker?

A. _____

B. _____

C. _____

3. What are three consequences when you get in an argument at work?

A. _____

B. _____

C. _____

4. What are three consequences of being mature enough to walk away from an argument at work?

A. _____

B. _____

C. _____

5. Why is it important to think in terms of consequences?

_____

_____

_____

_____

_____

_____

THE YOUNG AND THE GOAL-LESS
Les Brown

I was walking in the neighborhood one day with a classmate we called Brillo when some of the local tough guys who were members of the Fourteenth Street Gang yelled at me. "Hey, Les, we're gonna knock off a grocery store. You want to come along for the ride?"

I really didn't know if they were kidding or not. These were *rough* guys. They knew I was not into that sort of thing, but they kept hassling me. "What's the matter? You chicken? You a sissy?"

They got nowhere with me, so they laid into Brillo. He was not a close friend of mine, just a classmate, a guy from the neighborhood. Brillo did not have a lot going for him either at home or at school. He was more vulnerable to their taunts.

After they badgered him for a while, he gave them just what they'd been looking for. "I'm no chicken," he said. "I'll go, but I won't go inside. *I'll drive.*" He went with them. I went on to school. I didn't like being called a chicken but I cared more for how I thought about myself than for what those gang members thought of me.

I didn't look for Brillo on the way to school the next day. The morning newspapers told me where he was. The paper carried a full account of the robbery. When the robbers ran out, the store owner followed. He had a shotgun. He got a shot off into the car as it pulled away. Brillo was killed.

In many ways, I was not unlike Brillo. But I differed from him in one very significant way. My mother and Mr. Washington had helped fortify me against the pressures that led to Brillo's death. Thanks to their nurturing, I'd come to feel within myself that there were positive things in store for my life. Like most teenagers, I had my share of insecurities and fears, but I was comfortable and confident enough in myself that I resisted the gang's pressure to join them.

Cognition refers to the mental processes that include attention, remembering, producing and understanding language, solving problems, and making decisions.

MEMORY

1. Your memory is your responsibility, nobody else's. It is entirely within your scope to improve it. If your memory is poor and remains poor, it is because you can't be bothered to make it any better.

2. If you want to remember things, you've got to care about them.

3. The intellectual or academic memory is not an isolated structure: the more images and prompts you can bring in from the sensory memory, the better.

4. There is something compellingly mysterious about memory. It has fascinated scholars for centuries, and there is still much we do not know about it. As with any skill, a practical mixture of hard work, play, and sheer use will make an enormous difference. If you sincerely want to remember things, it's remarkable what you can do.

From *BRAIN TRAIN: STUDYING FOR SUCCESS,* Second Edition, by Richard Palmer, copyright © 1996 by Richard Palmer. Published by E & N Spon, an imprint of Chapman & Hall, London. Reprinted with permission from Taylor & Francis Books (UK).

THREE MAJOR WAYS OF LEARNING

| 1. REPETITION |
| 2. ASSOCIATION |
| 3. VISUALIZATION |

ARE YOU INTELLIGENT?

Thomas Armstrong

How intelligent are you? Chances are your answer to this question centers on tests and school-related skills. Maybe you've taken a ten-minute quiz in a popular magazine that involved solving problems like "x is to y as b is to __" or that asked you to provide the definitions to words such as *curmudgeon* and *mutafacient.* Perhaps you took an intelligence test in school or as a part of a job application. The concepts of IQ and intelligence exert a powerful hold on the imaginations of millions of Americans. To have a low IQ or to lack smarts in our society is to risk being labeled *retarded* or worse. In fact, many of our culture's grimiest epithets, including *moron, idiot,* and *imbecile,* were at one time regarded as scientifically correct ways of describing individuals who scored at the low end of the intelligence-testing curve. On the other hand, to be considered *gifted* or a *genius* (achieving an IQ score of 140 or more) is to enjoy the accolades of a society that provides perks for the best and brightest among *us:* Ivy League schools, advanced degrees, high incomes, and more. It's no wonder, then, that many of us still lie awake at night wondering what our IQ scores really are.

In ancient times, *everyone* was considered to possess inner genius. It was a kind of guardian spirit that accompanied a person through life and helped one overcome odds and achieve personal heights. We've lost touch with the original meaning of *genius* in our concern over IQ testing and similar nonsense.

In 1983, Howard Gardner proposed the theory of multiple intelligences to better describe the concept of intelligence and to account for a wider range of human potential in adults and children.

Gardner proposed eight basic types of intelligence, without claiming that this is a complete list.

Dr. Gardner states that our schools and culture focus most of their attention on linguistic and logical-mathematical intelligence. He claims that all humans have the right to be classified as intelligent, not just doctors and lawyers. A car mechanic, plumber, athlete, rapper, and a janitor are just as intelligent in their own right.

THE THEORY OF MULTIPLE INTELLIGENCES
THE EIGHT INTELLIGENCES
Howard Gardner

- Linguistic intelligence (word smart)

   The ability to understand and use words to clearly express yourself while speaking, writing, and reading.
   Careers:
   > Writer / Journalist
   > TV announcer
   > Lawyer
   > Teacher

- Logical-mathematical intelligence (number and reasoning smart)

   Has to do with logic, abstractions, reasoning, and numbers. Good at solving complex computations and excellent problem-solving skills.
   Careers:
   > Scientist
   > Engineer
   > Computer programmer
   > Mathematician

- Spatial intelligence (picture smart)

   Deals with spatial judgment and the ability to visualize. Recognizes patterns easily and good at interpreting pictures, graphs and charts.
   Careers:
   > Architect
   > Artist
   > Photographer
   > Interior decorator

- Musical intelligence (music smart)

   Has to do with sensitivity to sounds, rhythms, tones, and music. Recognizes musical patterns and tones, enjoy singing and playing musical instruments.
   Careers:
   > Musician
   > Singer
   > Music teacher
   > Disc jockey

- Interpersonal intelligence (people smart)

  The ability to get along with and to create positive relationships with others. Skilled at nonverbal communication. Good at resolving conflict in groups.

  Careers:

  > Psychologist
  > Nurse
  > Counselor
  > Sales person

- Intrapersonal intelligence (self-smart)

  Having a deep understanding of your strengths and weaknesses, what makes you unique, and being able to predict your own reactions and emotions

  Careers:

  > Philosopher
  > Teacher
  > Clergyperson
  > Scientist

- Naturalist intelligence (nature smart)

  Being able to classify natural forms such as animal and plant species, rocks and mountain types. Enjoys camping, gardening, hiking and exploring the outdoors

  Careers:

  > Biologist
  > Farmer
  > Gardener
  > Conservationist

- Bodily-kinesthetic intelligence (body smart)

  The ability to control of one's bodily motions skillfully and the capacity to handle objects skillfully. Good at dancing and sports.

  Careers:

  > Dancer
  > Athlete
  > Mechanic
  > Jeweler

A Native American elder once described his own inner struggles in this manner: Inside of me there are two dogs. One of the dogs is mean and evil. The other dog is good. The mean dog fights the good dog all the time. When asked which dog wins, he reflected for a moment and replied, "The one I feed the most.

—George Bernard Shaw (1856–1950)

THINKING SKILLS 74

All humans have a good side and a bad side. People are not just born good or born bad. It is a choice that we make. Good people have developed and are influenced by their inner good side, and bad people are influenced by their inner bad side. List five ways in which you feed the good side within yourself?

1. _____

_____

_____

2. _____

_____

_____

3. _____

_____

_____

4. _____

_____

_____

5. _____

_____

_____

WAYS TO DEVELOP THE GOOD WITHIN YOU

- Help other people.
- Control your thoughts and don't let your thoughts control you. Use positive self-talk.
- Use your mind and think before you act or react.
- Have confidence in yourself and your abilities.
- Accept responsibility for all of your actions.
- Become aware of your self-defeating behaviors.
- Always look for the good in other people and not the bad. Nobody is perfect.
- Block out negative thoughts.
- Treat all people with understanding, love, and respect. Be forgiving.
- Be patient, and don't assume life is easy.
- Do not compare yourself to others.
- Sacrifice immediate pleasures.
- Think win/win.
- Do not feel sorry for yourself.
- Set obtainable goals and stay focused.

GOAL SETTING

"Cheshire-Puss," she began, rather timidly, "would you tell me, please, which way I ought to go from here?"
"That depends a good deal on where you want to get to," said the cat.
"I don't much care where..." said Alice.
"Then it doesn't matter which way you go," said the cat.

—Alice in Wonderland

NO AIM

Our plans miscarry because they have no aim. When a man does not know what harbor he is making for, no wind is the right wind.

—Seneca (4 BC–65 AD)

GIVE ME A STOCK CLERK

Give me a stock clerk with a goal, and I will give you a man who will make history. Give me a man without a goal, and I will give you a stock clerk.

—J. C. Penney (1875–1971)

WHY FORMULATE GOALS?

Goals provide a sense of direction and a purpose for our actions. Without goals, you would not do anything and therefore not accomplish anything. Goals are the inspirations for our actions and direct us on which way to go. Goals are a map of how to specify, work toward, and achieve your own objectives.

PRIORITIES

Priorities are the things in your life that are the most important to you. You have to set and define your own priorities. Your future will be determined by your priorities and goals. If you do not have any priorities, do not expect a bright future. The decisions you make will not be consistent and will not create the kind of family, job, education, health, or friendships that you deserve.

Your list of priorities might look like this:
1. Family
2. Education
3. Meaningful work
4. Financial freedom
5. Health
6. Friendships
7. Faith
8. Lifestyle
9. Leisure pursuits
10. Influence
11. Travel
12. Helping others

GOALS AND OBJECTIVES
Colin Turner

Goals and objectives must be continuously decided upon and set. If you set a series of goals and reach all of them, then you must set new higher goals, for if you don't you can no longer be successful. If you have been a success in the past and possibly a big one but you no longer have an objective to attain then you cease to be successful. Also, if you have decided what your goals are, but do not work towards them, then you are not being successful. Finally, if you have set your goals and you are working towards them, but they are not worthwhile to you, then you are not being successful.

The important factor to understand is that any development of your untapped potential is a worthwhile goal. Success then is related to doing those things which you have not yet done and is not a comparison with what others have already done.

I believe that a major reason for people not achieving what they want is that they lack this clearly defined concept of what success is and that stems from the fact that although they may feel they want to succeed, they don't clearly define what they really want. They are consequently unable to know what they are able to achieve and therefore simply decide to stay as they are.

GOALS PROVIDE A TARGET

Goals provide a target to strive for and establish a framework around which other planning activities develop.

Goals:
1. Challenging but within reach
2. Specific
   (General goals can be used on a short-term basis.)
3. Measurable
4. Explicit (clearly and precisely understood)

Goal setting is an ongoing activity, and all of our effort should be directed toward reaching our goals. Our behavior and the decisions we make must be based on the goals we are working to achieve.

Goals can be developed for different areas of your life:
Family
Home
Financial
Career
Spiritual
Ethical
Health
Social
Educational

QUOTES FOR DISCUSSION

Concentrate all your thoughts upon the work at hand. The sun's rays do not burn until brought to a focus.

—Alexander Graham Bell (1847–1922)

He who every morning plans the transaction of the day and follows out that plan, carries a thread that will guide him through the maze of the most busy life. But where no plan is laid, where the disposal of time is surrendered merely to the chance of incidence, chaos will soon reign.

—Victor Hugo (1802–1885)

What this power is I cannot say; all I know is that it exists and it becomes available only when a man is in that state of mind in which he knows exactly what he wants and is fully determined not to quit until he finds it.

—Alexander Graham Bell (1847–1922)

Perhaps the most valuable result of all education is the ability to make yourself do the things you have to do, when it ought to be done, whether you like it or not. It is the first lesson that ought to be learned and however early a person's training begins, it is probably the last lesson a person learns thoroughly.

—Thomas H. Huxley (1825–1895)

Unless you try to do something beyond what you have already mastered, you will never grow.

—Ralph Waldo Emerson (1803–1882)

No one can cheat you out of ultimate success but yourself.

—Ralph Waldo Emerson (1803–1882)

THINKING SKILLS 75

1. What question can you never answer yes to?

   _____

2. There once was a horse
   That won great fame.
   What-do-you-think
   Was the horse's name.

   Can you name the horse?
   A. Yes   B. No   C. Not enough information

3. What do the following words have in common?

   deft, first, calmness, canopy, laughing, crab cake, hijack

   _____

4. How can you drop a raw egg onto a concrete floor without cracking it?

   _____

5. If you had three apples and four oranges in one hand and four apples and three oranges in the other hand, what would you have?

   _____

6. If it took eight men ten hours to build a wall, how long would it take four men to build it?

Question 2: *From THE COMPLETE THINKER: A HANDBOOK OF TECHNIQUES FOR CREATIVE AND CRITICAL PROBLEM SOLVING,* by Barry F. Anderson, copyright © 1980 by Prentice-Hall Inc. Published by Prentice-Hall, Inc. Reprinted with permission from Barry F. Anderson.

THINKING SKILLS 76

Write down your priorities and goals. Memorize your list of priorities, and use it as a guideline for everyday decision making. On a daily basis, examine how closely you are living your life according to you priorities and goals.

LIST YOUR PRIORITIES

My priorities are:

1._____

2._____

3._____

4._____

5._____

THINKING SKILLS 77

GOAL SETTING

Short-Term Goals

What do you want to accomplish within the next two years or less?

1._____

2._____

3._____

4._____

5._____

THINKING SKILLS 78

GOAL SETTING

Long-Term Goals
What do you want to accomplish within the next five years?

1._____

2._____

3._____

4._____

5._____

THINKING SKILLS 79

Do you have to change anything about your decision making or your lifestyle in order to reach your goals? Explain.

_____

_____

_____

_____

_____

_____

_____

_____

_____

_____

_____

_____

IT'S HARD TO
Jim Clemmer

It's hard to picture a positive, hopeful future if we're not positive and confident about ourselves. It's hard to see ourselves taking control of our destiny if we don't feel good about our own development, success, and skills.

Our self-vision or picture of ourselves is a major factor in our self-image. Years ago I heard the radio commentator and personal effectiveness speaker Earl Nightingale, say: "We become what we think about most."

What we think about and how we picture ourselves shows up in what we tell ourselves (and others) about us. Too often we excuse our performance or don't even bother trying because "I am not a speaker," "I am not a morning person," "I am disorganized," "I am not creative," "I am always late," "I am no good at paperwork," "I am not athletic," I am _____," (add your own).

These statements are the first step in a self-defeating, vicious cycle. The belief statement leads to a feeble attempt. That feeble attempt leads to poor results or failure. That in turn reinforces the original belief statement ("See! I told you I was no good at _____.")

It would be more accurate to say, "I've chosen to be disorganized," "I don't want to be creative," or "I don't think effective speaking is worth the effort."

If we want to change our personal output, we need to change the input. An important element in making personal effectiveness efforts work is changing your personal pictures and self-talk.

You aren't destined or stuck with any personal habits or characteristics. It's what you've chosen to become. Until you see your choices and change your self-vision, you will never become the high-performance leader you want or could be.

Statements we make to ourselves (our self-talk) have been called affirmations. Here are few of the affirmations I've used over the years: "I am a confident, compelling, and convincing speaker," "I love jogging and staying fit" (I hated it at the time), "We (the consulting company I was running) are flush with cash" (during a dark financial time), "I am a patient and loving father," and "Success is rolling in."

Affirmations keep you focused and true to your aim. They help "magnetize" you and your vision.

Put key affirmations tied to your vision in your day planner, on your desk, in your car, on your bathroom mirror—wherever you'll notice and repeat them. Supplement them with inspirational quotations on that theme or picture you're projecting. What you see is what you'll get.

Reprinted with permission from Jim Clemmer's (www.JimClemmer.com) bestseller *Pathways to Performance: A Guide to Transforming Yourself, Your Team, and Your Organization.*

See yourself and what you see you will become.
—Aristotle (384 BC–322 BC)

WHEN CHILDREN LEARN
David L. Weatherford

When children learn that happiness is not found in what a person has but in who that person is,

When they learn that giving and forgiving are more rewarding than taking and avenging,

When they learn that suffering is not eased by self-pity, but overcome by inner resolve and spiritual strength,

When they learn that they can't control the world around them, but they are the masters of their own souls,

When they learn that relationships will prosper if they value friendship over ego, compromise over pride, and listening over advising,

When they learn not to hate a person whose difference they fear, but to fear that kind of hate,

When they learn that there is pleasure in the power of lifting others up, not in the pseudo-power of pushing them down,

When they learn that praise from others is flattering but meaningless if it is not matched by self-respect,

When they learn that the value of a life is best measured not by the years spent accumulating possessions, but by the moments spent giving of one's self—sharing wisdom, inspiring hope, wiping tears and touching hearts,

When they learn that a person's beauty is seen not with the eyes but with the heart; and that even though time and hardships may ravage one's outer shell, they can enhance one's character and perspective,

When they learn to withhold judgment of people, knowing everyone is blessed with good and bad qualities, and that the emergence of either often depends on the help given or hurt inflicted by others,

When they learn that every person has been given the gift of a unique self, and the purpose of life is to share the very best of that gift with the world,

When children learn these ideals and how to practice them in the art of good living, they will no longer be children—they will be blessings to those who know them, and worthy models for all the world.

Reprinted with permission from Charlie Weatherford

THINKING SKILLS 80

1. A man is trapped in a room. The room has only two possible exits: two doors. Through the first door there is a room constructed from magnifying glass. The blazing-hot sun instantly fries anything or anyone that enters. Through the second door there is a fire-breathing dragon. How does the man escape?_____

2. If a man jumps out of a 68-story building window with no safety equipment or anything, how does he survive with not a scratch on him?_____

3. A man left his house to go to work. When he got home, he saw that his house had been broken into. The robbers had taken everything in his house except for two $100 bills that were in plain sight. Why weren't the $100 bills taken?

   _____

4. When things go wrong, what can you always count on?

   _____

5. Make one change to the following to make it into 6.

   ## IX

6. Two ducks in front of a duck, two ducks behind a duck, one duck in the middle. How many ducks are there?

   _____

LETTERS FROM PRISON

N.M.
Serving 55 years for murder

People who stand for nothing are easily bamboozled. I know because I once stood for nothing. A person who stands for nothing is like a used piece of furniture laying around in a yard unsecured during a storm. The wind comes along and throws the object around causing damage and threatening everything in its path. A person, on the other hand, who stands for nothing is easily bamboozled, misused, and exploited by those who recognize the shortcomings.

As I look back on my life, I am reminded of the traps along the way and how I got caught in those traps. Prior to my mid-thirties, I did not consciously embrace any principles, nor did I set any goals that were non-negotiable. Principles and goals are guides. They are like lighthouses that guide ships through the dark and turbulent sea. My principles and goals were spontaneously established depending on what was appealing and the opportunities available. I embraced and discarded principles like a disposal razor. As a result, I was often hoodwinked into anything because I stood for nothing. I was prey for drug addiction, peer pressure, conmen, schemes, criminal activities, etc. My behavior was not calculated. My behavior was dictated by the reality from which I functioned. I was ignorant.

QUOTES FOR DISCUSSION

The strong do what they have to do and the weak accept what they have to accept.

—Thucydides (460 BC–395 BC)

The longer we dwell on our misfortunes the greater is their power to harm us.

—Voltaire (1694–1778)

What wisdom can you find that is greater than kindness?

—Jean-Jacques Rousseau (1712–1778)

He is a wise man who does not grieve for the things which he has not, but rejoices for those which he has.

—Epicurus (341 BC–270 BC)

A wise man will make more opportunities than he finds.

—Sir Francis Bacon (1561–1626)

A bad beginning makes a bad ending.

—Euripides (484 BC–406 BC)

Many individuals have, like uncut diamonds, shining qualities beneath a rough exterior.

—Decimus Junius Juvenalis (55 AD–130 AD)

Associate yourself with people of good quality, for it is better to be alone than to be in bad company.

—Booker T. Washington (1856–1915)

Work is the grand cure of all the maladies and miseries that ever beset mankind.

—Thomas Carlyle (1795–1881)

When one door closes, another opens; but we often look so long and so regretfully upon the closed door that we do not see the one which has opened for us.

—Alexander Graham Bell (1847–1922)

SECTION 3

ORAL COMMUNICATION SKILLS

SECTION 3
ORAL COMMUNICATION SKILLS

Communication is the exchange of information between people by means of speaking, writing, or using a common system of symbols, signs, or behavior.

COMMUNICATION REQUIRES:

A sender

A message

An intended recipient

The communication process is complete once the receiver has understood the sender.

TYPES OF COMMUNICATION

Oral Communication

Oral communication is the process of using spoken words to successfully get your message across to others by conveying your thoughts and ideas effectively. The spoken verbal communication relies on words but also includes visual aids and nonverbal elements to assist the delivery of the meaning. Oral communication includes presentations, speeches, discussion, and other forms. In oral communication, body language and tone of voice can play a major role in getting your message across.

Nonverbal Communication

Nonverbal communication is the aspect of communication that does not involve verbal communication. It involves sending and receiving wordless messages. This includes facial expressions, body movements, eye contact, gestures, and posture. It is talking without speaking. Nonverbal elements are also included when using the spoken word. These elements include volume, voice quality, pitch, rate, and speaking style. Dance can be considered a form of nonverbal communication.

Written Communication

Written communication is communication by means of written symbols. It is the clear expression of ideas in writing and includes using correct grammar, spelling, and punctuation. The ideas must be expressed so the reader can understand them. Written communication is the most common form of business communication. This includes emails, memos, reports, and articles.

Visual Communication

Visual communication is the expression of information and ideas in forms that can be read or viewed. It is communication that relies on vision. Body language and gestures are part of this communication process. Visual communication can be expressed with images including drawings, designs, illustrations, and color. Other forms are video clips and television.

Workplace Oral Communication

- When receiving oral communication from a supervisor, the most important thing you can do is actively listen.
- Do not interrupt or disagree.
- Do not express disagreement through your body language.
- If you do not understand what you are being told, wait until the supervisor has finished before asking for clarification.
- Repeat the message in a nonthreatening tone to make sure you understand what you are being told.
- Let the supervisor communicate to you how he or she wants your job duties performed. Do not perform you job duties the way you think they should be performed. Your supervisor is the boss.

How to Be an Effective Workplace Communicator

- Be brief and to the point.
- Be friendly and non-confrontational.
- Make everyone feel special.
- Be coherent.
- Think before you speak.
- Be courteous.
- Do not put on a show to make a point.
- Do not become overly emotional.
- Don't talk too much.
- Speak slowly and with confidence.
- Make eye contact.
- Address people by name.
- Smile when appropriate.
- Use correct grammar.
- Stay focused on the message you are conveying.
- Keep it simple.

THINKING SKILLS 81

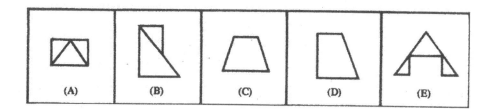

Find the simple figures (above) hidden in the more complex figures (below). Each figure has either A, B, C, D, or E hidden in it.

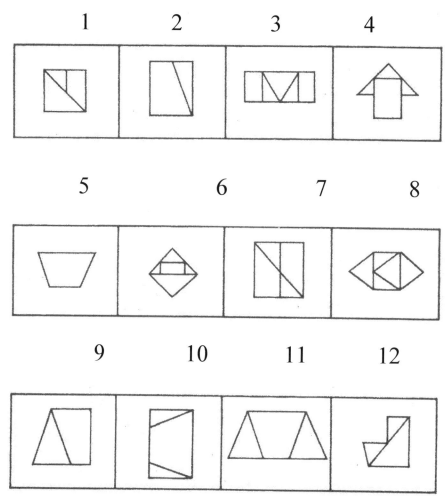

EMPLOYMENT NOTES

If you notice conditions that can be improved on a job, don't complain. Come up with a solution that will improve the conditions and effectively communicate the solution with your supervisor.

- Think before you speak.
- Your goal is to influence and persuade your supervisor to support your ideas. Be constructive.
- Give reasons why you think something can be improved.
- Think in terms of being able to save the company money.
- Propose improvements for the company benefit, not just your benefit.
- Use proper timing.
- Have a workable solution.
- Do not get defensive if your idea is not accepted.

PRINCIPLES OF COMMUNICATION

MOST PEOPLE REMEMBER
- 10 percent of what they read
- 20 percent of what they hear
- 30 percent of what they see
- 40 percent of what they hear and see

There's an old communications game, telegraph, that's played in a circle. A message is whispered around from person to person. What the exercise usually proves is how profoundly the message changes as it passes through the distortion of each person's inner "filter."

Communication is a two-way process of giving and receiving information through any number of channels. Whether one is speaking informally to a colleague, addressing a conference or meeting, writing a newsletter article or formal report, the following basic principles apply:

- Know your audience.
- Know your purpose.
- Know your topic.
- Anticipate objections.
- Present a rounded picture.
- Achieve credibility with your audience.
- Follow through on what you say.
- Communicate a little at a time.
- Present information in several ways.
- Develop a practical, useful way to get feedback.
- Use multiple communication techniques.

Communication is complex. When listening to or reading someone else's message, we often filter what's being said through a screen of our own opinions. One of the major barriers to communication is our own ideas and opinions.

From *PRINCIPLES OF COMMUNICATION*, Center for Urban Transportation Studies, University of Wisconsin-Milwaukee. Reprinted with permission from Edward A. Beimborn, Professor of Civil Engineering Emeritus.

> ## THE WAY YOU ASK A QUESTION CAN PROFOUNDLY INFLUENCE THE ANSWER YOU GET.

A young priest asked his bishop, "May I smoke while praying?" The answer was an emphatic "No!" Later, encountering an older priest puffing on a cigarette while praying, the younger priest scolded, "You shouldn't be smoking while praying! I asked the bishop, and he said I couldn't."

"That's strange," the older priest replied. "I asked the bishop if I could pray while smoking and he told me that it was okay to pray at any time."

From *SMART CHOICES: A PRACTICAL GUIDE TO MAKING BETTER DECISIONS,* by John S. Hammond, Ralph L. Keeney, and Howard Raiffa, copyright © 1999 by John S. Hammond, Ralph L. Keeney, and Howard. Published by Harvard Business School Press. Reprinted with permission from Harvard Business School Publishing.

NEGATIVE NONVERBAL COMMUNICATION SIGNALS COME FROM AN EMPLOYEE WHO:

- Is always late or missing work
- Has poor communication skills
- Needs constant supervision
- Never completes work assignments
- Is always arguing
- Is rude to customers and other employees
- Does not help other employees
- Has a not-caring attitude
- Has an unkempt work area
- Does less work than the other employees
- Never follows the rules
- Displays disruptive behavior
- Displays mean or disgustful facial expressions when given constructive criticism
- Roles his or her eyes when given a job assignment
- Displays a lack of caring for company equipment
- Cannot get along with other employees

POSITIVE NONVERBAL COMMUNICATION SIGNALS COME FROM AN EMPLOYEE WHO:

- Never misses work
- Is always on time
- Does not need supervision
- Completes work assignments
- Is mature enough not to argue
- Is never rude to customers and other employees
- Helps other employees
- Has a caring attitude
- Has a clean work area
- Does more work than what they are paid for
- Follows the rules
- Never displays disruptive behavior
- Displays a positive attitude when given constructive criticism
- Displays excellent listening skills
- Is considerate of company equipment
- Can get along with other employees
- Has good communication skills

THINKING SKILLS 82

List five examples of nonverbal communication that will give your supervisor the impression that you are not interested in your job.

1. _____

_____

2. _____

_____

3. _____

_____

4. _____

_____

5. _____

_____

THINKING SKILLS 83

Can you spot ten differences in butterfly B? Circle the differences.

A   **B**

QUOTES FOR DISCUSSION

It is better to keep your mouth closed and let people think you are a fool than to open it and remove all doubt.

—Mark Twain (1835–1910)

We have two ears and one mouth so that we can listen twice as much as we speak.

—Epictetus (55 AD–135 AD)

Be a craftsman in speech that thou may be strong, for the strength of one is the tongue, and speech is mightier than all fighting.

—Maxims of Ptahhotep (3400 BC)

If you are mighty, gain respect through knowledge and gentleness of speech.

—Maxims of Ptahhotep (3400 BC)

The fool who does not listen, can accomplish nothing at all. He sees knowledge as ignorance, usefulness as harmfulness.

—Maxims of Ptahhotep (3400 BC)

Be patient of heart the moment you speak, so as to say elevated things. In this way, the nobles who hear it will say: "How excellent and accomplished did he speak!"

—Maxims of Ptahhotep (3400 BC)

Speech is the mirror of the soul; as a man speaks, so is he.

—Publilius Syrus (first century BC)

True eloquence consists in saying all that is necessary, and nothing but what is necessary.

—Heinrich Heine (1797–1856)

One should aim not at being possible to understand, but at being impossible to misunderstand.

—Marcus Fabius Quintilianus (35 AD–100 AD)

Demosthenes overcame and rendered more distinct his inarticulate and stammering pronunciation by speaking with pebbles in his mouth.

—Plutarch (46 BC–199 BC)

There are few wild beasts more to be dreaded than a talking man having nothing to say.

—Jonathan Swift (1667–1745)

First learn the meaning of what you say, and then speak.
—Epictetus (55 AD–135 AD)

Talking and eloquence are not the same: to speak and to speak well are two things. A fool may talk, but a wise man speaks.
—Heinrich Heine (1797–1856)

Everyone may speak truly, but to speak logically, prudently, and adequately is a talent few possess.
—Michel de Montaigne (1553–1592)

To listen well is as powerful a means of communication and influence as to talk well.
—John Marshall (1755–1835)

Speaking with kindness creates confidence, thinking with kindness creates profoundness, giving with kindness creates love.
—Lao Tseu (sixth century BC)

Once a word has been allowed to escape, it cannot be recalled.
—Horace (65 BC–8 BC)

Words—so innocent and powerless as they are, as standing in a dictionary, how potent for good and evil they become, in the hands of one who knows how to combine them.
—Nathaniel Hawthorne (1804–1864)

ORGANIZATIONAL NORMS

Every company, no matter how large or small, has certain rules of behavior that all employees are required to follow. Companies expect all employees to act in a professional manner and to develop a professional work attitude. The purpose of these rules is not to confine the employee, but to create a more comfortable work atmosphere for all employees. To be successful on any job, you must be able to not let your private life interfere with the requirements of the organizational norms. Every person has room for improvement, and by developing good work habits, you can make your work more enjoyable and fulfilling.

Professional work behavior is reflected in an employee who:

- Has excellent communication skills
- Is dependable, trustworthy, and responsible
- Has a positive attitude and is a team player
- Does not require constant supervision
- Takes initiative
- Is not loud or disruptive
- Does not use drugs or alcohol
- Finds a solution rather than complains
- Does not use profane language
- Is considerate of other employees
- Is considerate of company property
- Constantly tries to improve
- Displays emotional control
- Helps other employees

After more than forty years of experience in the workplace, the one trait that I have noticed as being the main factor in people being hired for or promoted to management positions is communication skills. A lot of these people turned out to be very poor managers or supervisors, lacking management skills, most soft skills, leadership skills, and a general knowledge of the job. They got the position because they had excellent communication skills.

I have also witnessed the opposite: employees who would make excellent managers but were denied the opportunity because they lacked good communication skills.

THINKING SKILLS 84

1. Everyone can develop excellent communication skills.

    TRUE   FALSE

2. If you are a hard and dependable worker, you do not need good communication skills to get promoted.

    TRUE   FALSE

3. While communicating, I should say the first thing that comes to my mind.

    TRUE   FALSE

4. If I disagree with my supervisor, I should immediately argue my point.

    TRUE   FALSE

5. Communication is an exchange of ideas.

    TRUE   FALSE

6. Communication should allow you and your supervisor to understand each other better.

    TRUE   FALSE

7. Using phrases such as "You never…" or "You always…" or "Every time you…" only invites an argument.

    TRUE   FALSE

SIGNALS RECEIVED BY A MANAGER

SENDER: EMPLOYEE Signal Sent	RECEIVER: MANAGER Signal Received
Rolling eyes	Disagreement
Evil eye	Unfriendliness
Deep sigh	Not taking manager seriously
No eye contact	Suspicion
Not paying attention when being spoken to	Unfocused attention
Sour facial expressions	Displeasure
Crossing arms and leaning away	Employee thinks he or she is smarter than I am
Making the same mistake	Lack of interest
Not getting along with other employees	Lacks interpersonal skills
Argumentative	Not a team player
Poor work performance	Does not care
Mean expression	Avoid this employee
Talking during a meeting when the manager is talking	My opinion is not important to the employee
Always having to be told the same thing over and over	Poor listening skills
Sloppy work	Does not take pride in his or her work performance
Not dependable	Cannot be trusted
Poor communication skills	Do not promote

THINKING SKILLS 85

Each student should pick one topic, stand in front of the class, and talk about that topic for at least five minutes.

1. Can someone make you mad or angry?
2. What should you do if someone picks an argument with you at work?
3. Why is every job a good job?
4. What are five traits you can offer an employer?
5. Why are soft skills important?
6. What is maturity?
7. What are the main reasons employees get fired?
8. What are problems you might face on a new job?
9. What are some examples of soft skills?
10. Where do you want to be in ten years?
11. How has this class helped you?
12. What are your strengths?
13. What are areas in which you need to improve?
14. Why are communications skills important?
15. What is meant by being dependable?
16. Why should you always help other employees?
17. Why do employers not have time to babysit employees?
18. Why is adult life not easy?
19. How did Michael Jordan visualize?
20. How did Victor Frankl visualize?

SECTION 4

INTERPERSONAL AND TEAMWORK SKILLS

SECTION 4
INTERPERSONAL AND TEAMWORK SKILLS

Interpersonal skills are the skills used to properly interact and communicate with other people.

EXCELLENT WORKPLACE INTERPERSONAL SKILLS

- Talk with strangers and making them feel at ease
- Relating to supervisors and coworkers
- Interacting effectively with supervisors and coworkers
- Being nonjudgmental and respecting the opinions of others
- Having a positive attitude
- Not displaying angry or disgusting facial expressions
- Remaining cool and confident
- Not displaying disagreement through tone of voice
- Showing concern for others
- Making communication a two-way process
- Having the ability to listen
- Valuing the input of others and asking questions when confused
- Having positive body language
- Understanding that other employees' opinions will differ
- Thinking before speaking
- Not getting defensive
- Reducing conflict through excellent interpersonal skills
- Always thinking win/win
- Smiling

TEN WAYS TO IMPROVE YOUR INTERPERSONAL SKILLS

Are You Well Liked in the Office?

Interpersonal skills are invaluable at work. How your coworkers see you can have a big impact on your career long term, as well as on your day-to-day life. You may be the most brilliant person at your company, but if you can't get along with your colleagues, you won't get far. Fortunately, there are several things you can do to strengthen your social skills and become a team player. These ten actions will not only help you make better connections at work, they'll improve how others perceive you.

—Carrie Brenner

Tip #1: Put on a happy face.

People who are the life of the party usually have one thing in common: They're happy. If you smile often and have an upbeat attitude, your coworkers will be drawn to you. And when you're having a bad day, don't try to pull others down with you. You may find that people pass you by in favor of those with a more cheerful outlook.

Tip #2: Show that you care.

When it comes to praise, don't hold back the applause. If a coworker has done something you appreciate—no matter how small—thank them for it. Identify at least one attribute you value in each of your coworkers and let them know about it. Give colleagues a warm welcome whenever they call you or visit your office. By showing others how much you care about them, you'll encourage them to do the same in return and give you their best work.

Tip #3: Be considerate of colleagues.

Take note of what's happening with your coworkers. Recognize the happy events in their lives—from a birthday to a kid's kindergarten graduation—and be sure to show your genuine compassion when they face any personal tragedy. Look people in the eye when you speak to them, and refer to them using their first names. Show colleagues you value their input by asking their opinions.

Tip #4: Be an active listener.
Unfortunately, active listening is becoming a lost art. Being an active listener shows that you intend to both hear and recognize another's perspective. Using your own words, repeat what the speaker has said. By doing this, you'll know that you've processed their words, and they'll realize that your answers have been genuinely thought out. Colleagues will feel more connected to you knowing that you're an active listener, and you'll develop a better understanding of them.

Tip #5: Promote togetherness.
Help coworkers thrive by creating a friendly, cooperative environment. Treat everyone the same, not like they're part of a hierarchy, and don't act like one person's opinion is more important than another's. Don't gossip about your colleagues. Always consider your coworkers' suggestions. After addressing a crowd, make sure you've been understood. If you follow these rules, your coworkers will come to identify you as a team player and someone who can be trusted.

Tip #6: Settle disputes.
You know how to bring people together, and now it's time to become the person they can turn to when disputes arise. When colleagues disagree, it can bring the mood of the whole office down, but you can improve the situation by taking on the role of moderator. Arrange to have a discussion with both of the aggrieved parties, and try to help them resolve their conflict. Not only will your office be a happier place, but you'll come to be known as a leader.

Tip #7: Be a great communicator.
In addition to being an active listener, you need to have otherwise great communication skills. When in a discussion with colleagues, don't blurt out the first thing that comes to mind. Instead, think carefully about the words you use. With clear communication, you'll be able to avoid any

potential misunderstandings with colleagues. A good speaker comes to be known as intelligent and mature, no matter their age. If you have a tendency to give voice to any half-baked thought that crosses your mind, people won't put great value in your opinions.

Tip #8: Make them laugh.

Funny people are popular for a reason, so if you've got a great funny bone, use it. As long as you avoid inappropriate jokes and don't laugh off serious situations, you'll find your colleagues will be drawn to you. Humor can even be a great way to break down barriers with that super shy coworker or moody boss.

Tip #9: Put yourself in their shoes.

An empathetic person can understand how another person feels, and empathy is an important trait when working with others. Always consider circumstances from another person's viewpoint. What may seem like the obvious, correct answer to you could have entirely different implications when seen from another perspective. Above all, keep tabs on your own feelings; people who are unable to tap into their own emotions often have difficulty empathizing with others.

Tip #10: Don't be a whiner.

Almost every office has a chronic complainer, and you'll notice they tend to be the least popular person in the office. If you constantly whine about this and that, your negativity will push others away from you. If there's something you really need to get off your chest, write about it in your journal or briefly chat about it with your friends and family. Otherwise, you'll risk being known as the office brat.

Reprinted with permission from Fredric Paul, Editorial Director, AllBusiness.com
Source: www.allbusiness.com

PUT YOURSELF IN THEIR SHOES

I was working on a construction project in a wealthy neighbor. There were four of us on the crew. The owner of the house next to where we were working came outside and yelled at us for spilling some dirt on her lawn. She had a very negative attitude toward us, talked down to us, and was very mean, snobbish, and arrogant.

She went back inside and the four of us complained to each other about how we were treated and what we should have said back to her. I felt guilty for not responding to her.

To this day, I am very thankful that I did not respond to her comments and negative attitude. I sure wanted to.

After she went inside, a neighbor came over and explained to us that—two weeks earlier while her husband was home babysitting their nine-month-old son—the husband was doing laundry and did not notice when their son crawled outside through the open patio door, fell into the swimming pool, and drowned.

This experience has helped me to never respond to mean and negative people. Something is going on in their lives to make them act that way. I do not want to add to their problems and misery. It does not make me a better person to respond. It makes me a better person to let it come in one ear and go out the other.

THINKING SKILLS 86

1. What are interpersonal skills?

_____

_____

_____

2. List five ways in which you can display excellent interpersonal skills while at work.

A. _____

_____

B. _____

_____

C. _____

_____

D. _____

_____

E. _____

_____

3. Finish the following definition:
   Empathy means being able to _____

_____

_____

TOP 10 REASONS TO SMILE
Mark Stibich, Ph.D.

Smiling is a great way to make yourself stand out while helping your body to function better. Smile to improve your health, your stress level, and your attractiveness.

1. Smiling Makes Us Attractive

We are drawn to people who smile. There is an attraction factor. We want to know a smiling person and figure out what is so good. Frowns, scowls, and grimaces all push people away—but a smile draws them in.

2. Smiling Changes Our Mood

Next time you are feeling down, try putting on a smile. There's a good chance your mood will change for the better. Smiling can trick the body into helping you change your mood.

3. Smiling Is Contagious

When someone is smiling they lighten up the room, change the moods of others, and make things happier. A smiling person brings happiness with them. Smile lots and you will draw people to you.

4. Smiling Relieves Stress

Stress can really show up in our faces. Smiling helps to prevent us from looking tired, worn down, and overwhelmed. When you are stressed, take time to put on a smile. The stress should be reduced and you'll be better able to take action.

5. Smiling Boosts Your Immune System

Smiling helps the immune system to work better. When you smile, immune function improves possibly because you are more relaxed. Prevent the flu and colds by smiling.

6. Smiling Lowers Your Blood Pressure

When you smile, there is a measurable reduction in your blood pressure. Give it a try if you have a blood pressure monitor at home. Sit for a few minutes, take a reading. Then smile for a minute and take another reading while still smiling. Do you notice a difference?

7. Smiling Releases Endorphins, Natural Pain Killers and Serotonin

Studies have shown that smiling releases endorphins, natural pain killers, and serotonin. Together these three make us feel good. Smiling is a natural drug.

8. Smiling Lifts the Face and Makes You Look Younger

The muscles we use to smile lift the face, making a person appear younger. Don't go for a face lift, just try smiling your way through the day—you'll look younger and feel better.

9. Smiling Makes You Seem Successful

Smiling people appear more confident, are more likely to be promoted, and more likely to be approached. Put on a smile at meetings and appointments and people will react to you differently.

THINKING SKILLS 87

10. Smiling Helps You Stay Positive

Try this test: Smile. Now try to think of something negative without losing the smile. It's hard. When we smile, our body is sending the rest of us a message that "Life is good!" Stay away from depression, stress, and worry by smiling.

IT CAN BE DIFFICULT

It can be difficult to accept others and to accept ourselves. "I should be better. I should be something different. I should have more." All of this is conception; it's all mental fabrication. It's just the mind churning up "shoulds," "ought to's," and "supposed to's." All this is conceptual rubbish, and yet we believe it. Part of the solution is to recognize that these thoughts are conceptual rubbish and not reality; this gives us the mental space not to believe them. When we stop believing them, it becomes much easier to accept what we are at any given moment, knowing we will change in the next moment. We'll be able to accept what others are in one moment, knowing that they will be different in the next moment. This is good stuff for everyday practice; it's very practical.

HOW TO FREE YOUR MIND, TARA THE LIBERATOR, by Thubten Chodron, copyright © 2005 by Thubten Chodron. Published by Snow Lion Publication. Reprinted with permission from Snow Lion Publication.

EMPLOYMENT NOTES

When you are hired, you do not get to choose whom you work next to, and you do not get to choose your supervisors and managers. You will not be required to be friends with your fellow employees. You will be required to be mature enough and professional enough to get along with all of the other employees. You will have to learn to be respectful of others, even when you feel you are being disrespected. If you get in arguments, you and the other employee will eventually get fired. The choice you will have is to remain employed and accomplish your goals or be immature and get fired.

10 TYPES OF BAD SUPERVISORS

1. The Screamer
- Cannot handle pressure
- Thinks making employees fear for their jobs is a method of motivation
- Creates an unfriendly work environment
- Labels employees as troublemakers
- Lacks sensitivity for the employees
- They are harsh and abrasive

2. The Drill Sergeant Supervisor
- Wants employees to work hard but not smart
- Conditions employees not to take initiative, just wait for orders
- Maintains an attitude of "I am the boss and you have to listen to me"
- Thinks employee development requires being tough and hard
- Makes decisions without any employee input
- Manages by intimidation

3. The Win/Lose Supervisor
- Blames employees for mistakes but accepts little responsibility for anything
- Always blames employees for production problems which they have no control over and implies that it is their responsibility
- Tells employees that they have to "own it", but avoids making decisions
- Looks out for their own best interest and not the employees
- Waits until a project is finished to tell employees to do it a different way

4. The Think-They-Know-Everything-But-Knows-Nothing Supervisor
- Pays attention to small details, while major problems are overlooked
- Is insecure due to personal incompetence
- Tries to micro-manage in order to prove self-worth
- Sacrifices quality for presentation
- Creates more problems than they solve
- Is completely clueless and rarely produces results

5. The Teamwork-Destroyer Supervisor
- Does not understand the concept of teamwork
- Thinks they are the general manager, the coach, and the players all in one
- Treats employees like little kids and talks down to employees
- Talks about teamwork and trust but takes all the credit for employees' work and ideas
- Creates unhealthy competition among the employees
- Fails to recognize that the employees actually are very knowledgeable about their jobs

6. The "I–Will-Take-Care-Of-It" Supervisor
- Is friendly with great communication skills
- Does nothing but blows smoke
- Tells employees what they want to hear and then does not follow through
- Has no problem lying to employees or managers
- Gets no results and does nothing to solve employee problems
- Exaggerates personal work performance to superiors
- Does not support employees

7. The De-Motivator Supervisor
- Has no people skills
- Thinks a supervisor's job is to constantly tell employees how to do their jobs
- Will not recognize employees for outstanding performance
- Gives more work to capable employees and takes it away from those that are less capable
- Does not value employee input
- Has a bad attitude but expects employees to have a good attitude
- Is suspicious of employees

8. Earless Supervisor
- Has no listening skills
- Has the attitude of "I'm okay and you're not."
- Thinks they are better than the employees
- Talks a lot but doesn't remember what was said
- Takes ideas from employees, makes the ideas their own, and takes all of the credit
- Double-talks

9. The Terminator Supervisor
- Does not look for potential in employees
- Has no mentoring skills and will not help develop employees
- Thinks employees are not good enough if they make a mistake and figures they can hire somebody better
- Creates a low-production atmosphere with high turnover
- Unapproachable, over critical, and uses negative reinforcement

10. The It-Is-All-About-Me Supervisor
- Are not out for the good of the company or the employees
- Only care about themselves and getting ahead at the expense of the employees
- Sells out employees to make themselves look good
- Does not empower the employees because they do not want the employees to outperform them
- They consider employee suggestions as negative criticism
- Does not recognize dedicated employees (who actually make them look good)

EMPLOYMENT NOTES

Once you are employed, you will have contact with many different types of supervisors. Developing excellent interpersonal skills will help you to interact in a positive manner, even with the most negative and mean supervisors. Take a wider perspective and realize their behavior may not have anything to do with you. There are probably other causes for their behavior: problems at home, pressure from their boss, financial problems, or marital problems. Just because they are a supervisor does not mean they are perfect. When dealing with difficult people, don't take things personally. If you are being treated badly, they are usually treating a lot of other employees the same way. Bad supervisors usually never last. Still, it makes it much easier for you at work to stay on their good side.

EMPLOYMENT NOTES

If you don't like being told what to do, then take initiative and do things that need to be done. If your job is finished, go help another employee or find other work to do.

EMPLOYMENT NOTES

Face and solve your job-related problems. Changing jobs does not always solve problems. There is a good chance that you will experience the same problems on a new job. The problem is usually within the employee and not within the job.

THINKING SKILLS 88

1. Write down a four-letter word that is the same read forward, backward, or upside down.

   _____

2. Can you arrange 4 nines (9, 9, 9, 9) to total 100? You can use each nine only once.

   _____

3. Who was the last man to box Joe Louis?

   _____

4. Take two apples from five apples. How many do you have?

   _____

5. Why are 1988 pennies worth more than 1983 pennies?

   _____

6. What do you always get hanging from apple trees?

   _____

THINKING SKILLS 89

1. List five ways to improve interpersonal skills.

A. _____

_____

B. _____

_____

C. _____

_____

D. _____

_____

E. _____

_____

2. List five benefits of smiling.

A. _____

_____

B. _____

_____

C. _____

_____

D. _____

_____

E. _____

_____

A CREED TO LIVE BY

Nancye Sims

Don't undermine your worth by comparing yourself with others. It is because we are different that each of us is special.

Don't set your goals by what other people deem important. Only you know what is best for you.

Don't take for granted the things closest to your heart. Cling to them as you would your life, for without them, life is meaningless.

Don't let your life slip through your fingers by living in the past or for the future. By living your life one day at a time, you live all the days of your life.

Don't give up when you still have something to give. Nothing is really over until the moment you stop trying.

Don't be afraid to admit that you are less than perfect. It is this fragile thread that binds us to each together.

Don't be afraid to encounter risks. It is by taking chances that we learn how to be brave.

Don't shut love out of your life by saying it's impossible to find. The quickest way to receive love is to give; the fastest way to lose love is to hold it too tightly; and the best way to keep love is to give it wings.

Don't run through life so fast that you forget not only where you've been, but also where you are going.

Don't forget that a person's greatest emotional need is to feel appreciated.

Don't be afraid to learn. Knowledge is weightless, a treasure you can always carry easily.

Don't use time or words carelessly. Neither can be retrieved.

Life is not a race, but a journey to be savored each step of the way. Yesterday is History, Tomorrow is a Mystery and Today is a gift: that's why we call it—The Present."

Reprinted with permission from Nancye Sims

THANK YOU!

To those of you who laughed at me, thank you.
Without you I wouldn't have cried.

To those of you who just couldn't love me, thank you.
Without you I wouldn't have known real love.

To those of you who hurt my feelings, thank you.
Without you I wouldn't have felt them.

To those of you who left me lonely, thank you.
Without you I wouldn't have discovered myself.

But it is to those of you who thought I couldn't do it;
It is to you I thank the most,

Because without you I wouldn't have tried.

—Source Unknown, Author Unknown

I asked for Strength
And was given Difficulties to make me strong.
I asked for Wisdom
And was given Problems to solve.
I asked for Prosperity
And was given a Brain and Brawn to work.
I asked for Courage
And was given Danger to overcome.
I asked for Love
And was given Troubled people to help.
I asked for Favors
And was given Opportunities.
I received nothing I wanted. I received everything I needed.

—Source Unknown, Author Unknown

The most beautiful people I have known are those who have known defeat, known suffering, known struggle, known loss, and have found their way out of the depths. These people have an appreciation, a sensitivity and an understanding of life that fills them with compassion, gentleness, and a deep loving concern.

Beautiful people do not just happen.

—Dr. Kubler-Ross
Reprinted with permission from Ken Ross

Pain is a great teacher, but most of us would rather learn some other way. We think that happiness comes from a perfect childhood and avoiding mistakes. We don't like that patched up feeling that comes with each survival. We would like to be seamless—no patches, no scars. Cherish your hard-won depth and understanding that some pain is required for the journey. The gifts you seek are often disguised as problems.

Patches bring strength, whether on our knees or in our hearts.

—Dr. Jennifer James
Reprinted with permission from Jennifer James PhD

SHINING THROUGH THE TEARS
Irish Proverb

It's easy to be pleasant when life flows by like a song.
But the man worthwhile is the one who can smile
When everything goes dead wrong.

For the test of the heart is trouble
And it always comes with years.
And the smile that is worth the praises of earth
Is the smile that shines through the tears.

> # TEAMWORK
> Cooperative effort on the part of a group of people acting together in the interest of a common cause

WORKFORCE TEAMWORK SKILLS

- Do not judge others.
- Respect each individual worker and contribution.
- Be ready to comprise.
- Use clear communication.
- Know the common cause is for the good of the company and not the individual.
- Be willing to share information.
- Support and trust each other.
- Be willing to help other employees.
- Be responsible for the actions of the team.
- Perform duties even through conflict.

EMPLOYMENT NOTES

In the book *The Art of Happiness at Work* by the Dalai Lama and Howard C. Cutler, M.D., the Dalai Lama makes the following observation about the workplace environment:

One person can change the atmosphere of the workplace environment. You can see examples, for instance, of a very tense group of coworkers who don't get along, and then a new employee shows up, one who is warm and friendly, and after a while the mood and attitude of the whole group changes for the better. In the same way, sometimes you will see the opposite occur, where people at work are getting along and are friends, but then someone new will start work there, someone who is a troublemaker, and then that one can affect the whole group and cause conflicts and problems. So each of us can have an effect on others, and even change the atmosphere at work. And in that respect, a low-level worker might have more impact on one's immediate surroundings at work, at least in one's department, than the boss.

THINKING SKILLS 90

Each question consists of a numbered picture that shows the parts of an object. To the right of the numbered picture are several objects lettered A, B, C, and D. You are to select the lettered object that is made up from the numbered parts.

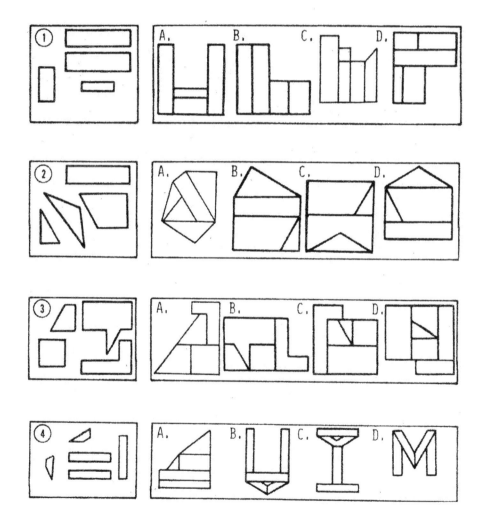

As human beings, we're not perfect, and we're not supposed to be.

But that's not always an easy thing for us to realize.

The best we can do is to do the best we can, give it our all, and always give thanks.

We don't make it alone in this world.

We're lucky that there are people placed in our path to guide us, protect us, and touch our lives so that we can get through it all...

one day at a time.

—Julia Escobar

FINAL NOTES

- Believe in yourself.

- Don't give up. Life is difficult.

- Develop the courage to follow your own path.

- Grow and mature through challenges.

- Overcome problems and troubles to gain strength.

- Constantly focus on your goals.

- Have the courage to be kind and considerate.

- Think before you act.

- Forego immediate pleasures.

- Do not let anger determine your outcome.

- Remember you can accomplish anything, but it takes time, focus, effort, and hard work.

- Realize your dreams through action.

- Smile

INDEX